295978

# DATE DUE

# A CHOICE OF
# CLOUGH'S VERSE

# A CHOICE OF CLOUGH'S VERSE

selected
with an introduction by
MICHAEL THORPE

FABER AND FABER
London

First published in this edition in 1969
by Faber and Faber Limited
24 Russell Square London W.C.1
Printed in Great Britain
by R. MacLehose and Company Limited
The University Press Glasgow
All rights reserved
© introduction by Michael Thorpe 1969
© this selection by Faber and Faber 1969

SBN (cloth edition) 571 08685 3
SBN (paper edition) 571 08686 1

# Contents

7

## *from* DIPSYCHUS

# Introduction

In an 1878 issue of *The Nation* a reviewer of the complete edition of the poems of Matthew Arnold wrote: 'it is to him [Arnold] and Clough that the men of the future will come who desire to find the clearest poetic expression of the sentiment and reflection of the most cultivated and thoughtful men of our generation.' This prophecy, as is the way of prophecies, has proved to have had a lop-sided truth. 'The men of the future' have indeed returned to Arnold, deluging him annually with books, theses and 'notes': Clough has had his place, more often than not, in the notes. He is habitually quoted as a footnote or appendix to a study of Arnold or of the Victorian period, usually imprisoned in the role of mid-Victorian 'Dipsychus', the conspicuous type of the divided, sceptical mind. As the prize product of Dr. Arnold's conscience-battery at Rugby, the tutor and friend of the great Matthew at Oxford and after, and as one who, despite his extraordinary promise, failed where his pupil flourished — in the great world itself — it is natural enough that he should have become the butt and foil of the Arnold Admiration Society. The members of this society, having scanned a few examples of Clough's drearier poems — assiduously quoted by their senior members and passed down unthinkingly through the generations — and having digested the Arnold letters to Clough, *not* the (regrettably lost) Clough letters to Arnold, have formed through sheer inertia a closed-shop against the shrewd, witty, delightful Clough:

'Thyrsis put up a fight, but all in vain. He lost: and from that day it has been Corydon, Corydon every time with us.'
(Virgil, *Eclogues*, VII, 69–70. Penguin trans.)

We can well understand why Thyrsis lost on Victorian pastures. What is surprising is his relative neglect in our time, despite one or two substantial efforts, whose effect seems to have been small, to revive interest when the centenary of his death came round in 1961.

9

Particularly significant has been the negative suggestion of such works as the influential *New Bearings in English Poetry* where, in a sweeping survey of the deficiencies of Victorian poetry and its unfitness to serve as a model for the moderns, F. R. Leavis racked Arnold and Browning, but didn't bother even to mention Clough. The minor French poets Corbière and Laforgue were, for Eliot and Pound, 'starting points such as were not to be found in English poetry of the nineteenth century': 'such as were not found' would have been more accurate, for, if there is a missing link between Eliot's admired Donne and Dryden and what we think of as modern poetry it is to be found — as Michael Roberts at least noted in his 1936 Introduction to *The Faber Book of Modern Verse* — in Clough.

If Eliot (like Dr. Leavis) seems to have known little about Clough, this seems to illustrate the force of the Clough Myth — an outstanding example of what Raymond Williams has called 'the selective tradition'. Almost as soon as Clough died in Florence, in his forty-third year, his reputation began to die with him. Within weeks, in the letters and obituaries of well-meaning but impercipient friends, the Clough Myth had been manufactured in a form that would last over a hundred years. This was nothing strange — throughout his life, as both man and poet, Clough suffered from a distorted interpretation of his virtues.

He was handicapped in the first place by his legendary triumphs at Rugby, where the reputation he built up for winning prizes, keeping goal and inspiring adulation in the breasts of the roughest young gentlemen was such as to make the *Boy's Own* seem tame fiction. He was the exception that proves Lytton Strachey's good rule that 'one must be commonplace to be a successful boy'. His tremendous all-round performance under the exacting Dr. Arnold, who was something of a father-figure to him — his family being in America, Clough had no regular home life during his Rugby days — severely taxed so naturally conscientious a boy. But the reaction gradually took effect during his Oxford period: when Rugby's hero came up to Balliol in 1837 he seemed to many to stand foremost among his generation,

Foremost one stood, with forehead high and broad, —

Sculptor n'er moulded grander dome of thought —
Beneath it, eyes dark-lustred rolled and glowed,
    Deep wells of feeling where the full soul wrought;

so began the commemorative poem 'Balliol Scholars' by Clough's
friend J. C. Shairp, but with the advantage of hindsight — it was
published in 1873 — the stanza ended,

Yet lithe of limb, and strong as shepherd's boy,
He roamed the wastes and drank the mountain joy,
    To cool a heart too cruelly distraught.

Clough failed, comparatively speaking, at Balliol. A 'certain
First', he managed only a Second in 'Literae Humaniores' and
failed to get a Balliol Fellowship. Though he recouped this in 1842
when, following in Dr. Arnold's footsteps, he was elected to an
Oriel Fellowship, it helped very little. Ever since he had come to
Oxford, at a time when the Tractarian controversy was in full
swing, his anxious intellect had been vexed by 'the vortex of
Philosophism and Discussion' about religion, which generated as
much heat amongst undergraduates as does the Vietnam War
today. He needed a breathing-space after his Rugby marathon and
freedom to think clearly, but his tutor, the Newmanite W. G.
Ward was, unfortunately, one of the sharpest logic-choppers in
the whole University. Continual contact with him and his kind
was 'the most exhausting exercise in the world. . . . I do not think
it can be wholly beneficial to anyone.' To Clough it certainly
wasn't and later Ward who, unlike Clough, did find a creed and
settled into Catholicism, regretted 'forcing' Clough's young mind;
Clough did eventually detach himself and 'Qua Cursum Ventus'
is probably an epitaph upon their relationship.

It is difficult today to imagine how radically the question of
owning or discarding orthodox religious belief could, in the mid-
Victorian period, disorientate a young man's life. In Clough's
case, the debate is not only a leading theme of his poetry — and an
endless one,

ACTION will furnish belief — but will that belief
    be the true one?
This is the point, you know          (*Amours*, Canto V)

11

— but it constantly intruded into the bread-and-butter side of his life. Because his religious doubts prevented him — unlike many less scrupulous contemporaries — from taking Holy Orders, which he would have had to do to hold his Oriel Fellowship beyond six years, he renounced the 'toga tutoria' in 1848, thus ending almost twenty years of cloistered intellectual fellowship at Rugby and Oxford to go out, as he wrote, into 'a wilderness, with small hope of manna, quails, or water from the rock'. He was never to find a better environment. His short-lived Principalship at University Hall, a hall of residence founded by Presbyterians and Unitarians for University College students of the new London University which, imposing no religious tests, might have suited him better, also foundered on religious rocks. While there, he dared not publish 'Amours de Voyage' or 'Easter Day' 'for fear of a row with my Sadducees' — the Hall's Management Committee. When, afterwards, he applied for a Chair at the new Sydney University College, the Provost of Oriel refused him a reference on the grounds that no one 'in a state of doubt or difficulty as to his own religious belief' was suitable for such a post; the Provost may also have been influenced by his notion that *The Bothie* was 'indelicate'. Clough didn't get the job.

After this, as the world saw it, he drifted and wasted his powers. Wishing to marry but lacking the means, and feeling deeply alienated from the English 'Establishment' — at Oxford he had compounded an unsavoury 'Republican' reputation with his agnosticism — he crossed the Atlantic to seek fortune and favour in a more liberal world:

> Come back, come back; and whither back or why?
> To fan quenched hopes, forsaken schemes to try;
> Walk the old fields; pace the familiar street;
> Dream with the idlers, with the base compete.

He had good American contacts, principally Emerson whom he had entertained in palmier days at Oxford (accompanying him to Paris after the 1848 Revolution) and he was soon on visiting terms with Lowell — his counterpart as a lively satirist — Longfellow and Charles Eliot Norton. He was lionized, even idealized; one admiring observer remembered how 'This handsome blonde

Englishman often passed Divinity Hall at Harvard on his way to visit the Nortons ... and he seemed to make more classic our pretty avenue.' But *plus ça change:* visiting cards were no substitute for dollars; Harvard Chairs were distributed on principles not dissimilar from those that held in the old country. Clough spent some months tutoring odds and ends of private pupils, devising half-hearted schemes for founding a dollar-spinning school — and sedulously avoiding the old religious arguments. He contracted his mind to the task work of revising Langhorne's bulky translation of Plutarch's *Lives* — 'not a religious subject fortunately,' he wrote.

Clough's fiancée, Blanche Smith, who was devotedly awaiting a call to join him, eventually grasped the fact that he would have to be shaken up or lost. When, through the influence of Clough's friends, an Examinership became available in the Education Office in London, she realized that this was perhaps the last chance of stability and an assured future for them: while he dithered in Cambridge (Mass.) she clinched the job and called him back. At the last moment he came, with misgivings, at length 'submitting', like Dipsychus, to conform and do a respectable, useful job, upholstered by an easeful family life such as he had never known. His last eight years were obscure and uneventful: he pushed the quill regularly, very often in letters to his American friends written on official notepaper; he was an affectionate and dutiful husband and father; he laboured at the 'plain work' of seeing through the press Florence Nightingale's (his wife's cousin) *Notes on Matters Affecting the Health Efficiency and Hospital Administration of the British Army* — this may have shortened his life; and he wrote virtually nothing, except, in his last sick months, the unfinished *Mari Magno*, largely the work of a broken man.

Thus summarized, it seems indeed a maimed life, brilliantly, perhaps too brilliantly, begun and fizzling out 'not with a bang but a whimper'. Such was the impression its obvious pattern made upon Clough's contemporaries, even upon his friends — but they, knowing and loving the man, sure that he had possessed great gifts yet finding too little evidence of these in his poetry, felt bound to apologize for him. Insisting warmly that he was more than he appeared to be, they only succeeded in confirming the myth of failure: 'Those who knew him well,' wrote Dean Stanley shortly after his death, 'know that in him a genius and character of no common order has passed away, but they will scarcely be able to justify their knowledge to a doubting world.' Recognizing that his public showing was unimpressive, they conspired to present him as one so abnormally high-principled that he could never act effectively, for action compels compromise. A sketch in one of the *Mari Magno* Tales provides a plausible self-portrait on these lines:

> He now, o'ertasked at school, a serious boy,
> A sort of after-boyhood to enjoy
> Appeared — in vigour and in spirit high
> And manly grown, but kept the boy's soft eye:
> And full of blood, and strong and light of limb,
> To him 'twas pleasure now to ride, to swim;
> The peaks, the glens, the torrents tempted him.
> Restless, it seemed, — long distances would walk,
> And lively was, and vehement in talk.
> A wandering life his life had lately been,
> Books he had read, the world had little seen.
> One former frailty haunted him, a touch
> Of something introspective overmuch.
> With all his eager motions still there went
> A self-correcting and ascetic bent,
> That from the obvious good still led astray,
> And set him travelling on the longest way. . . .

Unfortunately, Clough's friends made the life cover the poetry too, not recognizing how successfully in his poetry Clough could objectify his own 'negativism'. *Golden Treasury* Palgrave, in his 'Memoir' introducing *Poems* (1862) damned his old friend with this two-edged praise: 'It might be truly said that he rather lived than wrote his poem' — a remark that should have deterred potential readers from going far beyond the Memoir. The Myth was sealed, in a form that endures today for the many who read Arnold, not Clough, in Arnold's pastoral lament, 'Thyrsis: A Monody, to Commemorate the Author's Friend' —

> It irk'd him to be here, he could not rest.
> He loved each simple joy the country yields,
> He loved his mates; but yet he could not keep,

For that a shadow lour'd on the fields,
    Here with the shepherds and the silly sheep.
        Some life of men unblest
He knew, which made him droop, and fill'd his head.
    He went; his piping took a troubled sound
    Of storms that rage outside our happy ground;
He could not wait their passing, he is dead.

Here we have the simple, gentle Clough, the broken reed or, as
Humbert Wolfe put it, 'the shadowy Pierrot of a scholar-gipsy'.
Later in the poem Arnold dubs him, with phrase-making facility,
'too quick despairer,' and contrasts his 'golden prime' when his
music kept 'its happy country tone' — a fiction this, outside *The
Bothie* — with the later

stormy note

Of men contention-tost, of men who groan,
    Which task'd thy pipe too sore, and tired thy throat —
    It fail'd, and thou wast mute!

'Thyrsis', like 'Lycidas' and 'Adonais', is as much about the
elegist himself as his ostensible subject. Arnold's 'piping' also
'took a troubled sound' and he did admit privately that one motive
for treating Clough in this pastoral setting was his nostalgic desire
'to deal again with that Cumner country' (previously made
famous by his 'Scholar Gipsy'); there was also much in Clough
'which,' he said, 'one cannot deal with in this way.' That much is
the main: Clough's sharp intellect, his ample humour and his
singular imagination. But the damage was done and the Aunt
Sally set up for the younger gods, in their way, to shy at. There was
Swinburne in 1891: 'Literary history will hardly care to register
the fact that there was a bad poet named Clough, whom his
friends found it useless to puff: for the public, if dull, has not quite
such a skull as belongs to believers in Clough.' Then there was
the acidly epigrammatic Lytton Strachey, whose debunking books
on the earnest Victorians became primers of revolt for their grand-
children: in his *Eminent Victorians* sketch of Dr. Arnold Clough,
the formidable Rugby goal-keeper, the humorous celebrant in *The
Bothie* of 'the joy of eventful living', is set down in a few devastating

15

lines as the man with 'the weak ankles [true, but Clough was not defeated by them] and the solemn face', whose labours for Florence Nightingale's cause during his last years — which of course he should have devoted to the Muse — are hit off as a matter of 'parcels to be done up in brown paper and carried to the post.' One wonders if Strachey — who told a tribunal when he appeared before it, during the First World War, as a conscientious objector, that if he saw a German attempting to rape his sister he would try to get between them — had ever read this, in *Amours de Voyage*:

> Now supposing the French or the Neapolitan soldier
> Should by some evil chance come exploring the Maison Serny
> (Where the family English are all to assemble for safety),
> Am I prepared to lay down my life for the British female?
> Really who knows? . . .

Not that Clough can be claimed as Strachey's long-lost father — cynicism was never his metier — but there is an affinity, as with many another post-Victorian writer who probed the hollow postures of woman worship and *dulce et decorum*. Clough's Claude is certainly one of our first modern anti-heroes, if not *the* first; he was created in 1850.

Nevertheless, modern poets have not rushed to claim him as a forerunner, though they have singled out Browning and Hardy — and he belongs with these rather than with Tennyson or 'Corydon' Arnold. Perhaps accident to some extent accounts for this: though Clough's *Poems* sold well till about 1900, sales slackened off in the first decade of this century and the last 'Selection' appeared in 1910; after this, the next thing was the *Poems* of 1951, the first unbowdlerized edition. Thus we see that Clough dropped out of circulation, as it were, just at the time when English poetry was undergoing radical transformation. Pound and Eliot found French models, while Browning and Hardy, with their colloquial, often rugged style, were less sophisticated influences. Clough was nowhere, especially if the young poets of the day knew him — as they still do — as damnably 'earnest' and as a poet perhaps only through the invariably anthologized 'Say Not the Struggle Nought Availeth'. Besides, as this poem's mere title suggests, it must be admitted that Clough's diction is often archaic and he employs too frequent inversions and contracted forms. Yet this is a general Victorian vice, of which Clough is less guilty than most: every period has such drawbacks and we discount them if the poetry speaks to us in a more essential way.

It does speak to us, more directly than the style, at a superficial glance, may suggest. It is pointless today, when hardly anyone really reads Greek or Latin, to argue the toss about whether Clough was right to use hexameters in *The Bothie* and *Amours* and whether he used them rightly, questions that generated incredible heat in his day. Let us, with Charles Kingsley, call his hexameters 'Bothiaics', not travesties of the classical, and enjoy them as they deserve. Nor should it put us off that *Dipsychus* is rhymed throughout: the rhyme is varied in pattern and vigorous in tone — even its jingles serve a purpose, as they do in its model, Goethe's *Faust*.

Clough's appeal today is one of tone and substance. If, in Dr. Leavis's words, 'Poetry matters because of the kind of poet who is more alive than other people, more alive in his own age,' then Clough's poetry does matter (though the Doctor has overlooked it). It is a poetry that reflects a strong critical awareness of his own age, of what it meant then, in a world from which God seemed to have withdrawn, leaving it to be dominated by Mammon, to be acutely aware of the dilemma of *choice* where there no longer seemed to be any plain rights. It is the kind of situation that people now commonly find themselves in today and which has its best known literary expression in the early poems of T. S. Eliot. If, for Eliot, Prufrock's spiritual ancestors were the hesitant heroes of Laforgue, then Clough's Claude in *Amours de Voyage* may feel unjustly deprived of his posterity. Claude, the rightful ancestor, is appropriately riddled with scepticism and self distrust, a permanent onlooker at the battle of life or, in Clough's words, 'Spectator ab Extra'. Nowhere can he give himself ('I do not like being moved'); he is too self-engrossed, too inwardly divided to love; too perceptive of patriotic and political shams to fight — though, in his ironic heart, he is a republican. His underlying, undermining question is Prufrock's: 'Would it have been worthwhile . . .?' The clashing voices of the indecisive self can also be heard in the early poems of Tennyson, Arnold and Browning, but it is only in Clough that we hear the convincingly dramatized voice of modern ennui and (affected) indifference, dramatically controlled and ironically inflected.

Clough's power of control over his *personae* needs to be stressed. Whereas in some of the earlier *Ambarvalia* poems the subjective note had been strained, in *Amours* and *Dipsychus* he took care to avoid direct personal statement. In *Amours* he is in command of the full implications of his subject: it is a typical, not merely subjective, poem, as the Epilogue makes clear:

> Go, little book! . . .
> Go, and if curious friends ask of thy rearing and age,
> Say, 'I am flitting about many years from brain unto brain of
> Feeble and restless youths born to inglorious days. . . .

Doubtless there is much of Clough in Claude. In portraying him, he heightens his own admitted 'double mindedness' — and his equivocal attitude to the siege of the Roman Republic by the French in 1850, an experience that disillusioned him with 'our grand Lib. Eg. & Frat. Revolution' that only eighteen months before he had rushed to Paris to applaud is especially close — but the *story* is not autobiographical and the poem as a whole can be seen as a failure only in terms of the Clough Myth. The hero's — or anti-hero's — incapacity to act decisively does partly ally him with his creator, yet when Clough wrote the poem he had just taken bold action in cutting himself off from Oxford. Claude's disabling consciousness of the pros and cons of every question also resembles what Arnold called his friend's 'morbid conscientiousness', but in the poem Clough can see and ironically present Claude's behaviour *critically*. The process is similar to Goethe's deliberate turning of himself inside out to write *Werther* (though Clough, accused of 'Wertherism', said he had read most of it at twenty but 'didn't get to the end'). The poem's epigraphs point the deliberate intention at once (see p. 80). In Canto II we see how the hero's thoughts and feelings do indeed testify to a 'distempered appetite': he can rest in neither cynicism nor idealism; if, on the one hand, he mocks patriotism and 'woman worship', the next moment he is turning against Roman Republicanism (with which he basically sympathizes) or, again, mocking his self-preserving anti-heroic posture. Subtly, despite his critical detachment, his fifth letter to Eustace opens 'Yes we [not "they"] are fighting. . . .' Clough is no more Claude than Eliot is Prufrock.

Another strength of the poem is its psychological truth, in a way we appreciate more than Clough's contemporaries did, most of whom found it unpoetic and unhealthy. Even so sympathetic a friend as Emerson wrote, 'How can you waste such power on a broken dream? Why lead us up to the tower to tumble us down? . . . It is true, a few persons compassionately tell me, that the piece is all right, and that they like this veracity of much preparation to no result. But I hold 'tis bad enough in life, and inadmissable in poetry'. This was the kind of objection Clough — like Eliot or Forster, even sixty years after — was up against. Whereas the rather solemn Emerson, typical of his age, wanted wedding bells or suicide, the whole point of Clough's hero's failure — he ineptly pursues Mary Trevellyn halfway across Europe only to lose her at last — is that failure. 'I always meant it to be so,' Clough replied to Emerson, 'and began it with the full intention of it ending so.'

Early on Clough wrote to a friend that he didn't agree with 'the Painfulness and Martyrdom Poet-Theory' and this he held fast to, despite superficial appearances. His *Dipsychus* is no more a spun out piece of mere self-revelation than the *Amours* or *Don Juan* or his obvious model, Goethe's *Faust*: the witty Epilogue shows him fully aware of the poem's moral implications and of how the over-scrupulous mind portrayed in it, like yet unlike his own, came to be, and in what respects it was defective. But *Dipsychus* is still much misunderstood. 'Di-psychus': man of two natures or, in Clough's phrase, man with a 'double self'. This double self is *not* split, as a superficial reading might suggest, between Dipsychus and the Spirit — originally Dipsychus was called Faustulus (an apt diminutive) and the Spirit Mephistopheles; Dipsychus's dilemma resembles Faust's:

> Two souls, alas, cohabit in my breast,
> A contract one of them desires to sever.
> The one like a rough lover clings
> To the world with the tentacles of its senses;
> The other lifts itself to Elysian Fields
> Out of the mist on powerful wings.
>
> (Goethe's *Faust*, Part I. Trans. MacNeice & Stahl)

The Spirit is no crudely cut Tempter. Essentially he is *l'homme moyen sensuel*, whose realism and 'sense' are at one moment repellent, at another strikingly clear-sighted, as in the Lido scene a down-to-earth corrective to lofty idealism. He is the voice of one at home in the world, as Dipsychus — and Clough himself — could, somewhat regretfully, never be; he has the insidious appeal of the man of the world. He carries much of the poem's vitality, with a Byronic insouciance and an engaging irony; though Clough was hardly 'of the Spirit's party', he could put the more plausible side of the Spirit's viewpoint with sympathy, even with passion:

> To use the undistorted light of the sun
> Is not a crime; to look straight out upon
> The big plain things that stare one in the face
> Does not contaminate; to see pollutes not
> What one must feel if one won't see; what *is*. . . .
>
> (IX, 127–131)

Clough was not afraid of the, in Joyce's words, 'here and now, what you damn well have to see' — but putting it into poetry was no simple matter, living when he did.

Clough's social realism and satirical bite are unique in Victorian poetry. The realism embraces — figuratively speaking — prostitutes and pimps on the piazza and a respectable man's longing for one night of sin (*Dipsychus*, Scene IIA). On the satirical side there are scathing attacks on the ethics of *laissez faire* ('The Last Decalogue'), such hoary shibboleths as 'duty':

> Duty — that's to say complying
> With whate'er's expected here;

he inflates into an absurd jingle the comfortable middle-class notion that, society being ordered by God, we should rest content with the conditions to which it has pleased Him to call us:

> How pleasant it is to have money, heigh ho!
> How pleasant it is to have money.

His ruthless handling of sentimental woman worship and patriotism have already been mentioned, but a few lines cancelled in the *Amours* deserve resurrection:

O blessed government ours, blessed Empire of Purse and
    Policeman,
Fortunate islands of Order, Utopia of — breeches-pockets,
O happy England, and oh great glory of self-laudation.

The strongest — and saddest — satire, if it can be called that, is
'Easter Day' which, with its bitter echoes of some of Christianity's
most cherished texts ('catch not men, but fish'), voices more
intensely than any Victorian poem the anguish of the thwarted
believer. (Part II, the yea-saying sequel to this poem, omitted here,
is an unconvincing though typically Cloughian attempt at
dialectical balance.)

A good deal of what will now seem to have been remarkably
outspoken never met Victorian eyes. I have already mentioned
Clough's reluctance to publish *Amours* after its completion in
1849, for fear of offending his puritanical University Hall superiors:
it did not, in fact, appear till nine years later and then only in
America, in the ventursome Lowell's newly-founded *Atlantic
Monthly*. Some less guarded pieces have been printed only in our
day: lines 1–34 of 'O Land of Empire', in which priests spit and
sadly depraved dogs lift their legs against Roman remains while
boys follow suit in their own way, were only allowed to open the
poem in 1951; the whole of Scene IIA was omitted from the
Victorian version of *Dipsychus*, as also were these sharply pointed
and true lines from Scene V:

> Speak, outraged maiden, in thy wrong
> Did terror bring no secret bliss?
> Were boys' shy lips worth half a song
> Compared to the hot soldier's kiss?

Mrs. Clough had the jurisdiction over her husband's post-
humous *Poems*; how distasteful, sheltered middle class lady that
she was, she must have found this may be gauged from this
outburst — written after dipping, against Clough's express orders,
into the MSS. of *Dipsychus* while he was away in America:

'It is strange those peeps and reminders of your old times and
thoughts and your other sides always upset me — I believe I am
unjust. Now I am writing to you, it seems to come back to a more
usual state, but it is horrid — they seem to me full of honest coarse

21

strength and perception [a good critical observation!]. I don't mean to blame but I don't like it. I don't like men in general; I like women — why was not the world made all women — *can* there not be strength without losing delicacy. . . . I did hardly know that good men were so rough and coarse. I mean not that they prefer evil, but they consider of it so much — I do not mean anything about you — you always give me the impression of being good, very good.' —

It is a touching, almost propitiatory last sentence — perhaps Clough found it so. She must have found trying a lover who could, during their courtship, put straight down what Claude only thinks, for example: 'Your heart is a priceless treasure. No, I tell you, *it is not.*' She could even find the delightful 'Natura Naturans' 'abhorrent': though it had appeared in *Ambarvalia*, she managed to get it excluded from the first posthumous edition of the *Poems*, telling her co-editor that it was 'liable to great misconception' — perhaps that Clough had habitually committed mental adultery in second-class railway carriages? Which we find neither surprising nor shocking. In any case, she may have felt the unusual sexual potency of the imagery, for which one can find no parallel amongst Clough's contemporaries, nor later, till one comes to Lawrence's early poems. The dramatic situation and its psychological truth make the poem an anticipation of Hardy's lyrics that treat the subtleties of sexual attraction.

Clough is remarkably various in his treatment of sex and sexual relationships. If, on the one hand, he was willing — though without hope of publishing — to touch on what Mrs. Clough called the 'evil' side, on the other, in what he did publish, notably *The Bothie*, he treats the developing love between a man and a woman with tenderness and insight into the complicated elements of attraction and repulsion, desire and fear. Again one thinks of Lawrence who — more profoundly — had also a rare intuitive understanding of a woman's response. The noteworthy passages are in VII, beginning 'You are too strong, you see' and 'But a revulsion wrought in the brain and bosom of Elspie'. The imagery, one might say (perhaps mistakenly) is 'innocent', pre-Freudian, but is nonetheless true, intuitively rendered; for example, Elspie's dream of the bridge and the keystone of the arch:

Sometimes I dream of a great invisible hand coming down, and
Dropping the great key-stone in the middle : there in my
     dreaming,
There I feel the great key-stone coming in, and through it
Feel the other part — all the other stones of the archway,
Joined with mine with a strong, happy sense of completeness.

Elspie is the only 'pure maiden' one can think of in mid-
Victorian literature who is presented without mawkishness : and
this is chiefly because, in passages like that just quoted, Clough
understood what Charlotte Brontë had recently maintained in
*Jane Eyre*, that 'women feel as men feel' and that they can, however
gropingly, speak right out. This truth to feeling, together with
what Kingsley welcomed as its 'genial life' — of earnest, but not
too earnest, young men 'all in the glory of their shooting jackets',
constant fresh air playing upon their speculations, and 'lovely
potato-uprooters' with 'petticoats up to the knees, or even, it might
be, above them' — makes *The Bothie* unique, not just another
'modern poem' of sentiment on the lines laid down in Byron,
Goethe's *Herman and Dorothea* and, in the novel, George Sand's
*Jeanne*. The mock-heroic *Bothie* has more charm than any poem of
its time and more of the feel of contemporaneous life; it got its
warmest welcome in William Rossetti's review in *The Germ*, the
Pre-Raphaelite magazine devoted to 'Nature in Poetry, Literature
and Art'.

*The Bothie* represents the sunnier side of Clough's Oxford days,
when as a young don he used to lead Long Vacation reading
parties to the Scottish Highlands and the Lake District. Those
were not cloistered groups : Clough walked strenuously and, like
his hero, lodged in peasants' cottages; in a debate at Oxford on
'the character of a gentleman' he said, 'I have known peasant men
and women in the humblest places, in whom dwelt these qualities
as truly as ever they did in the best of lords and ladies, and who
were very poets of courtesy.' Hence his portraits of Elspie and her
father, not sentimental Rousseauesque fiction, but drawn from
experience and — allowing some licence of literacy — perfectly
convincing. In *The Bothie* Clough was, for once, thoroughly
'committed', and the whole long poem, with its lively, thinking

undergraduates, contains not a word of religious doubt. The tutor is not Clough entirely, but voices Clough's philosophy at its most restful: 'Grace is given of God, but knowledge is bought in the market.' The portly Hobbes has Clough's figure and humour; these lines referring to him were chosen by Mrs. Clough as apt to her husband:

Mute and exuberant by turns, a fountain at intervals playing,
Mute and abstracted, or strong and abundant as rain in the
    tropics;

Philip Hewson, the hero, is made, as Clough himself then was, a radical in sympathies — but a gentle light of irony plays over his and all the characterizations. Only near the end is the deeper note struck, in Philip's 'O that the armies indeed were arrayed' passage: small hope of this in the England of the 'forties so, like his real life model, Thomas Arnold the Younger, Philip packs off to New Zealand.

Something must be said of *The Bothie*'s strange title. Originally it was *The Bothie of Toper na Fuosich*, the title being related to the old name of a spot on the shores of Loch Ericht, but it was suggested in a review of the poem that it really referred to *Tobair na Feosag*, meaning 'the bearded well' — 'an ancient Highland toast to the female genital organs.' Though this interpretation has since been disputed, it naturally embarrassed Clough who thought the meaning had been 'the hut of the bairds' well' — or 'bairns' well' — he wasn't sure. Anyway, he had thought it vague and unfamiliar enough for his purpose: when he altered the title to its present form, he made it safely meaningless.

*The Bothie* seemed to promise that Clough would develop into a poet both bracing and cheerful, qualities not then combined in any but such 'parlour poets' as the monstrously popular Tupper. 'Tennyson', wrote Emerson, 'must look to his laurels' and Tom Arnold enthused from New Zealand, 'I feel now as if I could put entire trust, not only in your genius, but in your fortitude; about which alone I had formerly any doubts.' But the buoyant *Bothie* attitude to life, though fairly symptomatic, no doubt, of Clough's sense of relief just after cutting loose from Oxford, could not be sustained unimpaired. It is true that he impressed his contemporaries favourably with such things as 'The New Sinai', an attempt to square the New Science with essential Christianity, with 'Qui Laborat, Orat', a manly — if ascetic — devotional poem, and the invariably anthologized 'Say Not the Struggle Nought Availeth' (which Churchill invoked in 1940). But more often his tone was discomfiting: 'Doubt, it may be urged, is not a poet's mood,' wrote a reviewer of *Ambarvalia*, regretting that these poems, if generally emulated, 'will do more harm than good.'

Arnold was attacked in similar terms and responded by trying to write positively, treating 'great actions' of the past in such a way, though tragic, as 'to inspirit and rejoice'. Clough apparently felt that this was tricking out the truth in fancy dress: 'Not by turning and twisting his eyes', he wrote, 'in the hope of seeing things as Homer, Sophocles, Virgil, or Milton saw them; but by seeing them, by accepting them as he sees them, and faithfully depicting accordingly will he [the poet] attain the object he desires.' Arnold, on his part, was never quite fair to Clough either: he commended his efforts 'to get breast to breast with reality', but rated him for the 'deficiency of the *beautiful* in his poems'; though distinguished 'in the way of direct communication, insight, and report', Clough was *no artist*. Most Victorian readers would have been at one with Arnold in deploring Clough's lapses from the elevation of style which was the hallmark of the poet. For one thing he *thought* too much in poetry: Arnold thought too, so — sometimes — did Tennyson, but they expressed their thought more clearly and took more care to embroider it with the decorative arts of poetry. From Clough came such involved and witty metaphysics as 'Uranus' or the close of 'Look you, my simple friend' (beginning 'And can it be, you ask me'). Another offence was his refusal to treat poetry as soul-stuff, an attitude expressed with a lively disregard for euphony in 'Is it true ye gods'.

Though in theory he approved of poetry dealing with what Arnold shrugged away from — this 'unpoetical world' — welcoming and overrating the 'spasmodic' Alexander Smith for his 'images drawn from the busy seats of industry', there is disappointingly little such material in his own writing: but it is refreshing to us and it was something distinctive then that he could write of sexual attraction in a railway carriage ('Natura Naturans'), employ the image of a railway junction in a poem about human relationships ('Sic Itur') and, in *The Bothie* (IX) give an extended description of 'the whole great artificial civilized fabric' of a 'populous city' — albeit with a certain pre-Raphaelite glow. (The city would be Liverpool, his home town, rather than London.) But the glow of the romance transfigures, not denies, the underlying fact, for elsewhere he writes:

> At the huge members of the vast machine,
> In all those crowded rooms of industry,
> No individual soul has loftier leave
> Than fiddling with a piston or a valve.
>
> (*Dipsychus*, Sc. IX)

— a far from common insight then, in or out of poetry. Also, *The Bothie* is crammed with slang and colloquialisms of the day, which some Victorians thought 'unpoetical' and others delightfully refreshing — as is the irreverent (to 'Wordsworthian' Nature) description of his heroes' bathing in 'sparkling champagne' in 'Hobbes's gutter'.

In a period hostile to genuine satire (as Thackeray found), Clough was the strongest poetic satirist of the day — virtually the only one — largely because his mind was open, far-ranging, uncommitted to any such grand illusion as 'great' poets build on. He expresses the satirist's — and realist's — vital perception when he makes Dipsychus reject the ostrichism of those who,

> mark off thus much air
> And call it heaven, place bliss and glory there;
> Fix perfect homes in the unsubstantial sky. . . .

Instead: 'Let fact be fact, and life the thing it can.' In the middle of the bewildered nineteenth century, when writers searched for anodynes and felt it was their duty to provide them, he took Locke and Hume as masters of his thought and, like them, was prepared to follow where it led. We are more inclined to admire this quality of thought in poets today, to see it even as the *sine qua non* of the great poet. I should not care to assert Clough's 'greatness' — his creative imagination lacked amplitude and he left much of his poetry, including *Dipsychus*, unfinished — but, as Graham Greene has his hero in *The Quiet American* put it, 'He was an adult poet in the nineteenth century, there weren't so many of them.' Another, later, was Hardy — 'If Way to the Better there be, it exacts a full look at the Worst.' Perhaps most might feel that he falls short of greatness chiefly in his failure to reach

> High triumphs of convictions sought
> And won by individual thought
>
> ('O Happy They')

— unless what Jowett called his 'kind of faith in knowing nothing' is, in modern terms, a triumph.

That he never, as even Arnold, amongst others, persistently exhorted him to do, committed himself *against* his thought is certainly no mark of failure. Nor is it a mark of cynicism: he was never *happily* uncommitted, knowing well that 'Life loves no lookers-on at his great game' (*Dipsychus*, IX). He really learnt from Goethe that 'To act is easy, to think is hard'. Apart from *The Bothie*, written in 1848 in a mood of never-to-be-recovered freedom, his poetry thrived upon his inner divisions — as today we should expect — and most of his best work came out of two difficult years, 1849–50 ('I could have gone cracked at times last year with one thing or another' he wrote in 1851). Though his more disturbing poems had a mixed reception from his mid-century contemporaries, by 1882, in the increasingly agnostic climate of the late nineteenth century, Clough's one-time colleague at University Hall, R. H. Hutton, felt confident enough of his fame to prophesy: 'he will be ranked with Matthew Arnold, as having found a voice for this self-questioning age — a voice of greater range and richness even, and of a deeper pathos.' If in our time and in his own country — *American* criticism has done him justice — he has been seen in no such light, it has surely been because, from Dr. Leavis to the undergraduate with his handful of 'major authors', he has hardly been seen at all. My intention in making this selection has been to give him a belated fair chance of praise.


NOTE ON THE SELECTION

Clough's three principal poems, *The Bothie*, *Amours de Voyage* and *Dipsychus*, are too long for any one of them to be included entire in a

27

Selection of this kind. I have given about two thirds of *The Bothie*, together with brief interlinking summaries of the omitted portions to maintain the thread of action, about a third of *Amours* — one of the longest of its five cantos plus a substantial part of another — and two thirds of *Dipsychus*, Clough's most remarkable poem.

The text is based on *The Poems of Arthur Hugh Clough*, edited by H. P. Lowry, A. L. P. Norrington and F. L. Mulhauser (Oxford: Clarendon Press, 1951). I have departed from it in these respects: (1) to facilitate reading I have given every poem a title, though often there is none in the Oxford *Poems*; where these titles are not Clough's, I have simply used the first line or opening words of the poem or what I think are the more appropriate of the many titles supplied by Clough's earliest editors, his wife and John Addington Symonds; (2) I have given 'Natura Naturans' as Clough revised it, not as it was first printed in *Ambarvalia*, while 'A London Idyll' is as Clough copied it into a letter recently printed in *New Zealand Letters of Thomas Arnold the Younger* (Ed. J. Bertram, Oxford 1967) — this was evidently a careful fair copy and is, in literary terms, superior to the one the Oxford editors give; (3) the Catullus translation has been taken from the Bodleian MSS., as printed by Lady Katharine Chorley in her *Arthur Hugh Clough, the Uncommitted Mind*; (4) and lastly, I have included as a whole Scene IIA of *Dipsychus*, large sections of which were relegated to their Notes by the Oxford editors in an attempt 'to preserve the general sense and the best poetry'. So much of Clough's work was left unfinished that there seems little point in any particular case in trying to polish it for him. Other notably 'unfinished' pieces in this Selection, in the section 'Shorter Poems (II)' are: 'Were You With Me', and 'But That From Slow Dissolving Pomps of Dawn'.

I am grateful to the Clarendon Press for permission to include certain poems and passages that were published for the first time in 1951.

Since this is not intended to be an annotated selection, I have restricted footnotes to a very few points of especial interest or difficulty.

Michael Thorpe
*Leiden*
*March 1968*

# THE SHORTER POEMS (I)

From *Ambarvalia* (1849)

## *The Questioning Spirit*

The human spirits saw I on a day,
Sitting and looking each a different way;
And hardly tasking, subtly questioning,
Another spirit went around the ring
To each and each: and as he ceased his say,
Each after each, I heard them singly sing,
Some querulously high, some softly, sadly low,
We know not, — what avails to know?
We know not, — wherefore need we know?
This answer gave they still unto his suing,
We know not, let us do as we are doing.

Dost thou not know that these things only seem? —
I know not, let me dream my dream.
Are dust and ashes fit to make a treasure? —
I know not, let me take my pleasure.
What shall avail the knowledge thou hast sought? —
I know not, let me think my thought.
What is the end of strife? —
I know not, let me live my life.
How many days or e'er thou mean'st to move? —
I know not, let me love my love.
Were not things old once new? —
I know not, let me do as others do.
And when the rest were over past,
I know not, I will do my duty, said the last.

Thy duty do? rejoined the voice,
Ah do it, do it, and rejoice;
But shalt thou then, when all is done,
Enjoy a love, embrace a beauty
Like these, that may be seen and won
In life, whose course will then be run;
Or wilt thou be where there is none?
I know not, I will do my duty.

And taking up the word around, above, below,
Some querulously high, some softly, sadly low,
We know not, sang they all, nor ever need we know!
We know not, sang they, what avails to know?
Whereat the questioning spirit, some short space,
Though unabashed, stood quiet in his place.
But as the echoing chorus died away
And to their dreams the rest returned apace,
By the one spirit I saw him kneeling low,
And in a silvery whisper heard him say:
Truly, thou know'st not, and thou need'st not know:
Hope only, hope thou, and believe alway;
I also know not, and I need not know,
Only with questionings pass I to and fro,
Perplexing these that sleep, and in their folly
Imbreeding doubt and sceptic melancholy;
Till that, their dreams deserting, they with me
Come all to this true ignorance and thee.

## Sic Itur

As, at a railway junction, men
Who came together, taking then
One the train up, one down, again

Meet never! Ah, much more as they
Who take one street's two sides, and say
Hard parting words, but walk one way:

Though moving other mates between,
While carts and coaches intervene,
Each to the other goes unseen,

Yet seldom, surely, shall there lack
Knowledge they walk not back to back,
But with a unity of track,

Where common dangers each attend,
And common hopes their guidance lend
To light them to the self-same end.

Whether he then shall cross to thee,
Or thou go thither, or it be
Some midway point, ye yet shall see

Each other, yet again shall meet.
Ah, joy ! when with the closing street,
Forgivingly at last ye greet !


## Qui Laborat, Orat

O only Source of all our light and life,
    Whom as our truth, our strength, we see and feel,
But whom the hours of mortal strife
    Alone aright reveal !

Mine inmost soul, before Thee inly brought,
    Thy presence owns ineffable, divine ;
Chastised each rebel self-encentered thought,
    My will adoreth Thine.

With eye down-dropt, if then this earthly mind
    Speechless remain, or speechless e'en depart ;
Nor seek to see — for what of earthly kind
    Can see Thee as Thou art ? —

If well-assured 'tis but profanely bold
    In thought's abstractest forms to seem to see,
It dare not dare the dread communion hold
    In ways unworthy Thee,

O not unowned, Thou shalt unnamed forgive,
    In worldly walks the prayerless heart prepare;
And if in work its life it seem to live,
    Shalt make that work be prayer.

Nor times shall lack, when while the work it plies,
    Unsummoned powers the blinding film shall part,
And scarce by happy tears made dim, the eyes
    In recognition start.

But, as thou willest, give or e'en forbear
    The beatific supersensual sight,
So, with Thy blessing blest, that humbler prayer
    Approach Thee morn and night.


## The New Sinai

Lo, here is God, and there is God!
    Believe it not, O Man;
In such vain sort to this and that
    The ancient heathen ran:
Though old Religion shake her head,
    And say in bitter grief,
The day behold, at first foretold,
    Of atheist unbelief:
Take better part, with manly heart,
    Thine adult spirit can;
Receive it not, believe it not,
    Believe it not, O Man!

As men at dead of night awaked
    With cries, 'The king is here,'
Rush forth and greet whome'er they meet,
    Whoe'er shall first appear;
And still repeat, to all the street,
    ''Tis he, — the king is here;'
The long procession moveth on,
    Each nobler form they see
With changeful suit they still salute,
    And cry, ''Tis he, 'tis he!'


So, even so, when men were young,
    And earth and heaven was new,
And His immediate presence He
    From human hearts withdrew,
The soul perplexed and daily vexed
    With sensuous False and True,
Amazed, bereaved, no less believed,
    And fain would see Him too:
He is! the prophet-tongues proclaimed;
    In joy and hasty fear,
He is! aloud replied the crowd,
    Is here, and here, and here.


He is! They are! in distance seen
    On yon Olympus high,
In those Avernian woods abide,
    And walk this azure sky:
They are, They are! to every show
    Its eyes the baby turned,
And blazes sacrificial, tall,
    On thousand altars burned:
They are, they are! — On Sinai's top
    Far seen the lightnings shone,
The thunder broke, a trumpet spoke,
    And God said, I am One.

God spake it out, I, God, am One;
  The unheeding ages ran,
And baby-thoughts again, again,
  Have dogged the growing man:
And as of old from Sinai's top
  God said that God is One,
By Science strict so speaks He now
  To tell us, There is None!
Earth goes by chemic forces; Heaven's
  A Mécanique Céleste!
And heart and mind of human kind
  A watch-work as the rest!

Is this a Voice, as was the Voice
  Whose speaking told abroad,
When thunder pealed, and mountain reeled,
  The ancient Truth of God?
Ah, not the Voices; 'tis but the cloud,
  Of outer darkness dense,
Where image none, nor e'er was seen
  Similitude of sense.
'Tis but the cloudy darkness dense
  That wrapt the Mount around;
While in amaze the people stays,
  To hear the Coming Sound.

Is there no chosen prophet-soul
  To dare, sublimely meek,
Within the shroud of blackest cloud
  The Deity to seek?
'Midst atheistic systems dark,
  And darker hearts' despair,
His very word it may have heard,
  And on the dusky air
His skirts, as passed He by, to see
  Have strained on their behalf,
Who on the plain, with dance amain,
  Adore the Golden Calf.

'Tis but the cloudy darkness dense;
　　Though blank the tale it tells,
No God, no Truth! yet He, in sooth,
　　Is there — within it dwells;
Within the sceptic darkness deep
　　He dwells that none may see,
Till idol forms and idol thoughts
　　Have passed and ceased to be:
No God, no Truth! ah though, in sooth
　　So stand the doctrine's half;
On Egypt's track return not back,
　　Nor own the Golden Calf.

Take better part, with manlier heart,
　　Thine adult spirit can;
No God, no Truth, receive it ne'er —
　　Believe it ne'er — O Man!
But turn not then to seek again
　　What first the ill began;
No God, it saith; ah, wait in faith
　　God's self-completing plan;
Receive it not, but leave it not,
　　And wait it out, O Man!

'The Man that went the cloud within
　　Is gone and vanished quite;
He cometh not,' the people cries,
　　'Nor bringeth God to sight:'
'Lo these thy gods, that safety give,
　　Adore and keep the feast!'
Deluding and deluded cries
　　The Prophet's brother-Priest:
And Israel all bows down to fall
　　Before the gilded beast.

Devout, indeed! that priestly creed,
　　O Man, reject as sin;

The clouded hill attend thou still,
    And him that went within.
He yet shall bring some worthy thing
    For waiting souls to see:
Some sacred word that he hath heard
    Their light and life shall be;
Some lofty part, than which the heart
    Adopt no nobler can,
Thou shalt receive, thou shalt believe,
    And thou shalt do, O Man!


## The Poet

Look you, my simple friend, 'tis one of those
(Alack, a common weed of our ill time),
Who, do whate'er they may, go where they will,
Must needs still carry about the looking-glass
Of vain philosophy. And if so be
That some small natural gesture shall escape them,
(Nature will out) straightway about they turn,
And con it duly there, and note it down,
With inward glee and much complacent chuckling,
Part in conceit of their superior science,
Part in forevision of the attentive look
And laughing glance that may one time reward them,
When the fresh ore, this day dug up, at last
Shall, thrice refined and purified, from the mint
Of conversation intellectual
Into the golden currency of wit
Issue — satirical or pointed sentence,
Impromptu, epigram, or it may be sonnet,
Heir undisputed to the pinkiest page
In the album of a literary lady.

    And can it be, you ask me, that a man,
With the strong arm, the cunning faculties,

And keenest forethought gifted, and, within,
Longings unspeakable, the lingering echoes
Responsive to the still-still-calling voice
Of God Most High, — should disregard all these,
And half-employ all those for such an aim
As the light sympathy of successful wit,
Vain titillation of a moment's praise?
Why, so is good no longer good, but crime
Our truest, best advantage, since it lifts us
Out of the stifling gas of men's opinion
Into the vital atmosphere of Truth,
Where He again is visible, tho' in anger.

## The Clouded Hill

Sweet streamlet bason! at thy side
Weary and faint within me cried
My longing heart, — In such pure deep
How sweet it were to sit and sleep;
To feel each passage from without
Close up, — above me and about,
Those circling waters crystal clear,
That calm impervious atmosphere!
There on thy pearly pavement pure
To lean, and feel myself secure,
Or through the dim-lit inter-space,
Afar at whiles upgazing trace
The dimpling bubbles dance around
Upon thy smooth exterior face;
Or idly list the dreamy sound
Of ripples lightly flung, above
That home, of peace, if not of love.

# From 'Blank Misgivings of a Creature Moving in Worlds not Realized'*

### I

Here am I yet, another twelvemonth spent,
One-third departed of the mortal span,
Carrying on the child into the man,
Nothing into reality. Sails rent,
And rudder broken, — reason impotent, —
Affections all unfixed; so forth I fare
On the mid seas unheedingly, so dare
To do and to be done by, well content.
So was it from the first, so is it yet;
Yea, the first kiss that by these lips was set
On any human lips, methinks was sin —
Sin, cowardice, and falsehood; for the will
Into a deed e'en then advanced, wherein
God, unidentified, was thought-of still.

### III

Well, well, — Heaven bless you all from day to day!
Forgiveness too, or e'er we part, from each,
As I do give it, so must I beseech:
I owe all much, much more than I can pay;
Therefore it is I go; how could I stay
Where every look commits me to fresh debt,
And to pay little I must borrow yet?
Enough of this already, now away!
With silent woods and hills untenanted
Let me go commune; under thy sweet gloom,
O kind maternal Darkness, hide my head:
The day may come I yet may re-assume
My place, and, these tired limbs recruited, seek
The task for which I now am all too weak.

*The title is taken from Wordsworth's 'Ode: Intimations or Immortality . . .'

— Like a child
In some strange garden left awhile alone,
I pace about the pathways of the world,
Plucking light hopes and joys from every stem,
With qualms of vague misgiving in my heart
That payment at the last will be required,
Payment I cannot make, or guilt incurred,
And shame to be endured.

X

I have seen higher holier things than these,
   And therefore must to these refuse my heart,
Yet am I panting for a little ease;
   I'll take, and so depart.

Ah hold! the heart is prone to fall away,
   Her high and cherished visions to forget,
And if thou takest, how wilt thou repay
   So vast, so dread a debt?

How will the heart, which now thou trustest, then
   Corrupt, yet in corruption mindful yet,
Turn with sharp stings upon itself! Again,
   Bethink thee of the debt!

— Hast thou seen higher holier things than these,
   And therefore must to these thy heart refuse?
With the true best, alack, how ill agrees
   That best that thou wouldst choose!

The Summum Pulchrum rests in heaven above;
   Do thou, as best thou may'st, thy duty do:
Amid the things allowed thee live and love;
   Some day thou shalt it view.

# Qua Cursum Ventus*

As ships, becalmed at eve, that lay
   With canvas drooping, side by side,
Two towers of sail at dawn of day
   Are scarce long leagues apart descried;

When fell the night, upsprung the breeze,
   And all the darkling hours they plied,
Nor dreamt but each the self-same seas
   By each was cleaving, side by side:

E'en so — but why the tale reveal
   Of those, whom, year by year unchanged,
Brief absence joined anew, to feel
   Astounded, soul from soul estranged?

At dead of night their sails were filled,
   And onward each rejoicing steered —
Ah, neither blame, for neither willed,
   Or wist, what first with dawn appeared!

To veer, how vain! On, onward strain,
   Brave barks! In light, in darkness too,
Through winds and tides one compass guides —
   To that, and your own selves, be true.

But O blithe breeze! and O great seas,
   Though ne'er, that earliest parting past,
On your wide plain they join again,
   Together lead them home at last.

One port, methought, alike they sought,
   One purpose hold where'er they fare, —
O bounding breeze, O rushing seas!
   At last, at last, unite them there!

* The title is from Virgil, *Aeneid III, 269.*

# Natura Naturans

Beside me, — in the car, — she sat,
  She spake not, no, nor looked to me:
From her to me, from me to her,
  What passed so subtly stealthily?
As rose to rose that by it blows
  Its interchanged aroma flings;
Or wake to sound of one sweet note
  The virtues of disparted strings.

Beside me, nought but this! — but this,
  That influent as within me dwelt*
Her life, mine too within her breast,
  Her brain, her every limb she felt:
We sat; while o'er and in us, more
  And more, a power unknown prevailed,
Inhaling, and inhaled, — and still
  'Twas one, inhaling or inhaled.

Beside me, nought but this; — and passed;
  I passed; and know not to this day
If gold or jet her girlish hair,
  If black, or brown, or lucid-grey
Her eye's young glance: the fickle chance
  That joined us, yet may join again;
But I no face again could greet
  As hers, whose life was in me then.

Touched not, nor looked; yet owned we both
  The Power which e'en in stones and earths
By blind elections felt, in forms
  Organic breeds to myriad births;
By lichen small on granite wall
  Approved, its faintest feeblest stir

* A notebook version of this line runs: That as within my body
dwelt.

Slow-spreading, strengthening long, at last
   Vibrated full in me and her.

In me and her — sensation strange !
   The lily grew to pendent head,
To vernal airs the mossy bank
   Its sheeny primrose spangles spread,
In roof o'er roof of shade sun-proof
   Did cedar strong itself outclimb,
And altitude of aloe proud
   Aspire in floreal crown sublime;

Flashed flickering forth fantastic flies,
   Big bees their burly bodies swung,
Rooks roused with civic din the elms,
   And lark its wild reveillez rung;
In Libyan dell the light gazelle,
   The leopard lithe in Indian glade,
And dolphin, brightening tropic seas,
   In us were living, leapt and played:

Their shells did slow crustacea build,
   Their gilded skins did snakes renew,
While mightier spines for loftier kind
   Their types in amplest limbs outgrew;
Yea, close comprest in human breast,
   What moss, and tree, and livelier thing,
What Earth, Sun, Star of force possest,
   Lay budding, burgeoning forth for Spring.

Such sweet preluding sense of old
   Led on in Eden's sinless place
The hour when bodies human first
   Combined the primal prime embrace,
Such genial heat the blissful seat
   In man and woman owned unblamed,
When, naked both, its garden paths
   They walked unconscious, unashamed:

Ere, clouded yet in mistiest dawn,
    Above the horizon dusk and dun,
One mountain crest with light had tipped
    That Orb that is the Spirit's Sun;
Ere dreamed young flowers in vernal showers
    Of fruit to rise the flower above,
Or ever yet to young Desire
    Was told the mystic name of Love.


## Is it True, Ye Gods

Is it true, ye gods, who treat us
As the gambling fool is treated,
O ye, who ever cheat us,
And let us feel we're cheated!
Is it true that poetical power,
The gift of heaven, the dower
Of Apollo and the Nine,
The inborn sense, 'the vision and the faculty divine,'
All we glorify and bless
In our rapturous exaltation,
All invention, and creation,
Exuberance of fancy, and sublime imagination,
All a poet's fame is built on,
The fame of Shakespeare, Milton,
Of Wordsworth, Byron, Shelley,
Is in reason's grave precision,
Nothing more, nothing less,
Than a peculiar conformation,
Constitution, and condition
Of the brain and of the belly?
Is it true, ye gods who cheat us?
And that's the way ye treat us?

Oh say it, all who think it,
Look straight, and never blink it!

If it is so, let it be so,
And we will all agree so;
But the plot has counterplot,
It may be, and yet be not.


# From *The Bothie of Tober-na-Vuolich*

## A LONG-VACATION PASTORAL

### I

*Socii cratera coronant*\*

It was the afternoon; and the sports were now at the ending.
Long had the stone been put, tree cast, and thrown the hammer;
Up the perpendicular hill, Sir Hector so called it,
Eight stout gillies had run, with speed and agility wondrous;
Run too the course on the level had been; the leaping was over:
Last in the show of dress, a novelty recently added,
Noble ladies their prizes adjudged for costume that was perfect,
Turning the clansmen about, as they stood with upraised elbows,
Bowing their eye-glassed brows, and fingering kilt and sporran.
It was four of the clock, and the sports were come to the ending,
Therefore the Oxford party went off to adorn for the dinner.
  Be it recorded in song who was first, who last, in dressing.
Hope was first, black-tied, white-waistcoated, simple, His Honour;
For the postman made out he was heir to the Earldom of Ilay,
(Being the younger son of the younger brother, the Colonel),
Treated him therefore with special respect; doffed bonnet, and ever
Called him his Honour: his Honour he therefore was at the
      cottage.
Always his Honour at least, sometimes the Viscount of Ilay.
  Hope was first, his Honour, and next to his Honour the Tutor.
Still more plain the Tutor, the grave man, nicknamed Adam,
White-tied, clerical, silent, with antique square-cut waistcoat

* Virgil, *Georgics II*, l. 528.

44

Formal, unchanged, of black cloth, but with sense and feeling
     beneath it;
Skilful in Ethics and Logic, in Pindar and Poets unrivalled;
*Shady* in Latin, said Lindsay, but *topping* in Plays and Aldrich.
  Somewhat more splendid in dress, in a waistcoat work of a lady,
Lindsay succeeded; the lively, the cheery, cigar-loving Lindsay,
Lindsay the ready of speech, the Piper, the Dialectician,
This was his title from Adam because of the words he invented,
Who in three weeks had created a dialect new for the party;
This was his title from Adam, but mostly they called him the
     Piper.
Lindsay succeeded, the lively, the cheery, cigar-loving Lindsay.
  Hewson and Hobbes were down at the *matutine* bathing; of
     course too
Arthur, the bather of bathers *par excellence*, Audley by surname,
Arthur they called him for love and for euphony; they had been
     bathing,
Where in the morning was custom, where over a ledge of granite
Into a granite bason the amber torrent descended,
Only a step from the cottage, the road and larches between them.
Hewson and Hobbes followed quick upon Adam; on them
     followed Arthur.
  Airlie descended the last, effulgent as god of Olympus;
Blue, perceptibly blue, was the coat that had white silk facings,
Waistcoat blue, coral-buttoned, the white-tie finely adjusted,
Coral moreover the studs on a shirt as of crochet of women:
When the fourwheel for ten minutes already had stood at the
     gateway,
He, like a god, came leaving his ample Olympian chamber.
  And in the fourwheel they drove to the place of the clansmen's
     meeting.
  So in the fourwheel they came; and Donald the innkeeper
     showed them
Up to the barn where the dinner should be. Four tables were in it;
Two at the top and the bottom, a little upraised from the level,
These for Chairman and Croupier, and gentry fit to be with them,
Two lengthways in the midst for keeper and gillie and peasant.
Here were clansmen many in kilt and bonnet assembled:

45

Keepers a dozen at least; the Marquis's targeted gillies;
Pipers five or six, among them the young one, the drunkard;
Many with silver brooches, and some with those brilliant crystals
Found amid granite-dust on the frosty scalp of the Cairn-Gorm;
But with snuff-boxes all, and all of them using the boxes.
Here too were Catholic Priest, and Established Minister standing;
Catholic Priest; for many still clung to the Ancient Worship,
And Sir Hector's father himself had built them a chapel;
So stood Priest and Minister, near to each other, but silent,
One to say grace before, the other after the dinner.
Hither anon too came the shrewd, ever-ciphering Factor,
Hither anon the Attaché, the Guardsman mute and stately,
Hither from lodge and bothie in all the adjoining shootings
Members of Parliament many, forgetful of votes and blue-books,
Here, amid heathery hills, upon beast and bird of the forest
Venting the murderous spleen of the endless Railway Committee.
Hither the Marquis of Ayr, and Dalgarnish Earl and Croupier,
And at their side, amid murmurs of welcome, long-looked for,
    himself too
Eager, the grey, but boy-hearted Sir Hector, the Chief and the
    Chairman.
  Then was the dinner served, and the Minister prayed for a
    blessing,
And to the viands before them with knife and with fork they beset
    them;
Venison, the red and the roe, with mutton; and grouse succeeding;
Such was the feast, with whisky of course, and at top and bottom
Small decanters of Sherry, not overchoice, for the gentry.
So the viands before them with laughter and chat they beset them.
And, when on flesh and on fowl had appetite duly been sated,
Up rose the Catholic Priest and returned God thanks for the
    dinner.
Then on all tables were set black bottles of well-mixed toddy,
And, with the bottles and glasses before them, they sat, digesting,
Talking, enjoying, but chiefly awaiting the toasts and speeches.
  Spare me, O great Recollection! for words to the task were
    unequal,
Spare me, O mistress of Song! nor bid me remember minutely

46

All that was said and done o'er the well-mixed tempting toddy;
How were healths proposed and drunk 'with all the honours,'
Glasses and bonnets waving, and three-times-three thrice over,
Queen, and Prince, and Army, and Landlords all, and Keepers;
Bid me not, grammar defying, repeat from grammar-defiers
Long constructions strange and plusquam-Thucydidean,
Tell how, as sudden torrent in time of speat* in the mountain
Hurries six ways at once, and takes at last to the roughest,
Or as the practised rider at Astley's or Franconi's
Skilfully, boldly bestrides many steeds at once in the gallop,
Crossing from this to that, with one leg here, one yonder,
So, less skilful, but equally bold, and wild as the torrent,
All through sentences six at a time, unsuspecting of syntax,
Hurried the lively good-will and garrulous tale of Sir Hector.
Left to oblivion be it, the memory, faithful as ever,
How the Marquis of Ayr, with wonderful gesticulation,
Floundering on through game and mess-room recollections,
Gossip of neighbouring forest, praise of targeted gillies,
Anticipation of royal visit, skits at pedestrians,
Swore he would never abandon his country, nor give up deer-
    stalking;
How, too, more brief, and plainer in spite of the Gaelic accent,
Highland peasants gave courteous answer to flattering nobles.
    Two orations alone the memorial song will render;
For at the banquet's close spake thus the lively Sir Hector,
Somewhat husky with praises exuberant, often repeated,
Pleasant to him and to them, of the gallant Highland soldiers
Whom he erst led in the fight; — somewhat husky, but ready,
    though weary,
Up to them rose and spoke the grey but gladsome chieftain: —
    Fill up your glasses, my friends, once more, — With all the
    honours!
There was a toast I forgot, which our gallant Highland homes have
Always welcomed the stranger, delighted, I may say, to see such
Fine young men at my table — My friends! are you ready? the
    Strangers.

* Flood (Clough's note).

47

Gentlemen, here are your healths, — and I wish you — With all
  the Honours!
    So he said, and the cheers ensued, and all the honours,
All our Collegians were bowed to the Attaché detecting his
  Honour,
Guardsman moving to Arthur, and Marquis sidling to Airlie,
And the small Piper below getting up and nodding to Lindsay.
  But, while the healths were being drunk, was much tribulation
    and trouble,
Nodding and beckoning across, observed of Attaché and
  Guardsman:
Adam wouldn't speak, — indeed it was certain he couldn't;
Hewson could, and would if they wished; Philip Hewson a poet,
Hewson a radical hot, hating lords and scorning ladies,
Silent mostly, but often reviling in fire and fury
Feudal tenures, mercantile lords, competition and bishops,
Liveries, armorial bearings, amongst other matters the Game-laws:
He could speak, and was asked-to by Adam, but Lindsay aloud
  cried
(Whisky was hot in his brain), Confound it, no, not Hewson,
A'nt he cock-sure to bring in his eternal political humbug?
However, so it must be, and after due pause of silence,
Waving his hand to Lindsay, and smiling oddly to Adam,
Up to them rose and spoke the poet and radical Hewson.
  I am, I think, perhaps the most perfect stranger present.
I have not, as have some of my friends, in my veins some tincture,
Some few ounces of Scottish blood; no, nothing like it.
I am therefore perhaps the fittest to answer and thank you.
So I thank you, sir, for myself and for my companions,
Heartily thank you all for this unexpected greeting,
All the more welcome, as showing you do not account us intruders,
Are not unwilling to see the north and the south forgather.
And, surely, seldom have Scotch and English more thoroughly
  mingled;
Scarcely with warmer hearts, and clearer feeling of manhood,
Even in tourney, and foray, and fray, and regular battle,
Where the life and the strength came out in the tug and tussle,
Scarcely, where man met man, and soul encountered with soul, as

48

Close as do the bodies and twining limbs of the wrestlers,
When for a final bout are a day's two champions mated, —
In the grand old times of bows, and bills, and claymores,
At the old Flodden-field — or Bannockburn — or Culloden.
— (And he paused a moment, for breath, and because of some
        cheering,)
We are the better friends, I fancy, for that old fighting,
Better friends, inasmuch as we know each other the better,
We can now shake hands without pretending or shuffling.
  On this passage followed a great tornado of cheering,
Tables were rapped, feet stamped, a glass or two got broken:
He, ere the cheers died wholly away, and while still there was
        stamping,
Added, in altered voice, with a smile, his doubtful conclusion.
  I have, however, less claim than others perhaps to this honour,
For, let me say, I am neither game-keeper, nor game-preserver.
  So he said, and sat down, but his satire had not been taken.
Only the *men*, who were all on their legs as concerned in the
        thanking,
Were a trifle confused, but mostly sat down without laughing;
Lindsay alone, close-facing the chair, shook his fist at the speaker.
Only a Liberal member, away at the end of the table,
Started, remembering sadly the cry of a coming election,
Only the Attaché glanced at the Guardsman, who twirled his
        moustachio,
Only the Marquis faced round, but, not quite clear of the meaning,
Joined with the joyous Sir Hector, who lustily beat on the table.
  And soon after the chairman arose, and the feast was over:
Now should the barn be cleared and forthwith adorned for the
        dancing,
And, to make way for this purpose, the tutor and pupils retiring
Were by the chieftain addressed and invited to come to the castle.
But ere the door-way they quitted, a thin man clad as the Saxon,
Trouser and cap and jacket of homespun blue, hand-woven,
Singled out, and said with determined accent to Hewson,
Touching his arm: Young man, if ye pass through the Braes o'
        Lochaber,
See by the loch-side ye come to the Bothie of Tober-na-vuolich.

## II

*Et certamen erat, Corydon cum Thyrside, magnum*\*

Morn, in yellow and white, came broadening out from the
    mountains,
Long ere music and reel were hushed in the barn of the dancers.
Duly in *matutine* bathed before eight some two of the party,
Where in the morning was custom, where over a ledge of granite
Into a granite bason the amber torrent descended.
There two plunges each took Philip and Arthur together,
Duly in *matutine* bathed, and read, and waited for breakfast:
Breakfast, commencing at nine, lingered lazily on to noon-day.
    Tea and coffee were there; a jug of water for Hewson;
Tea and coffee; and four cold grouse upon the sideboard;
Gaily they talked, as they sat, some late and lazy at breakfast,
Some professing a book, some smoking outside at the window.
By an aurora soft-pouring a still sheeny tide to the zenith,
Hewson and Arthur, with Adam, had walked and got home by
    eleven;
Hope and the others had staid till the round sun lighted them
    bedward.
They of the lovely aurora, but these of the lovelier women
Spoke — of noble ladies and rustic girls, their partners.
    Turned to them Hewson, the chartist, the poet, the eloquent
    speaker.
Sick of the very names of your Lady Augustas and Floras
Am I, as ever I was of the dreary botanical titles
Of the exotic plants, their antitypes, in the hot-house:
Roses, violets, lilies for me! the out-of-door beauties;
Meadow and woodland sweets, forget-me-nots and heartsease!
    Pausing awhile, he proceeded anon, for none made answer.
Oh, if our high-born girls knew only the grace, the attraction,
Labour, and labour alone, can add to the beauty of women,
Truly the milliner's trade would quickly, I think, be at discount,
All the waste and loss in silk and satin be saved us,
Saved for purposes truly and widely productive —
                                That's right,

\* Virgil, *Eclogues*, VII, l. 16.

Take off your coat to it, Philip, cried Lindsay, outside in the
    garden,
Take off your coat to it, Philip.
                              Well, then, said Hewson, resuming;
Laugh if you please at my novel economy; listen to this, though;
As for myself, and apart from economy wholly, believe me,
Never I properly felt the relation between men and women,
Though to the dancing-master I went, perforce, for a quarter,
Where, in dismal quadrille, were good-looking girls in abundance,
Though, too, school-girl cousins were mine — a bevy of
    beauties, —
Never, (of course you will laugh, but of course all the same I shall
    say it,)
Never, believe me, I knew of the feelings between men and women,
Till in some village fields in holidays now getting stupid,
One day sauntering 'long and listless,' as Tennyson has it,
Long and listless strolling, ungainly in hobbadiboyhood,
Chanced it my eye fell aside on a capless, bonnetless maiden,
Bending with three-pronged fork in a garden uprooting potatoes.
Was it the air? who can say? or herself, or the charm of the labour?
But a new thing was in me; and longing delicious possessed me,
Longing to take her and lift her, and put her away from her slaving.
Was it embracing or aiding was most in my mind? hard question!
But a new thing was in me, I, too, was a youth among maidens:
Was it the air? who can say? but in part 't was the charm of the
    labour.
Still, though a new thing was in me, the poets revealed themselves
    to me,
And in my dreams by Miranda, her Ferdinand, often I wandered,
Though all the fuss about girls, the giggling, and toying, and
    coying,
Were not so strange as before, so incomprehensible purely;
Still, as before (and as now), balls, dances, and evening parties,
Shooting with bows, going shopping together, and hearing them
    singing,
Dangling beside them, and turning the leaves on the dreary piano,
Offering unneeded arms, performing dull farces of escort,
Seemed like a sort of unnatural up-in-the-air balloon-work,

(Or what to me is as hateful, a riding about in a carriage,)
Utter removal from work, mother earth, and the objects of living.
Hungry and fainting for food, you ask me to join you in snapping —
What but a pink-paper comfit, with motto romantic inside it?
Wishing to stock me a garden, I'm sent to a table of nosegays;
Better a crust of black bread than a mountain of paper confections,
Better a daisy in earth than a dahlia cut and gathered,
Better a cowslip with root than a prize carnation without it.
   That I allow, said Adam.

                              But he, with the bit in his teeth, scarce
Breathed a brief moment, and hurried exultingly on with his rider,
Far over hillock, and runnel, and bramble, away in the champaign,
Snorting defiance and force, the white foam flecking his flanks, the
Rein hanging loose to his neck, and head projecting before him.


   Oh, if they knew and considered, unhappy ones! oh, could they
      see, could
But for a moment discern, how the blood of true gallantry kindles,
How the old knightly religion, the chivalry semi-quixotic
Stirs in the veins of a man at seeing some delicate woman
Serving him, toiling — for him, and the world; some tenderest
      girl, now
Over-weighted, expectant, of him, is it? who shall, if only
Duly her burden be lightened, not wholly removed from her, mind
      you,
Lightened if but by the love, the devotion man only can offer,
Grand on her pedestal rise as urn-bearing statue of Hellas; —
Oh, could they feel at such moments how man's heart, as into Eden
Carried anew, seems to see, like the gardener of earth uncorrupted,
Eve from the hand of her Maker advancing, an helpmeet for him,
Eve from his own flesh taken, a spirit restored to his spirit,
Spirit but not spirit only, himself whatever himself is,
Unto the mystery's end sole helpmate meet to be with him; —
Oh, if they saw it and knew it; we soon should see them abandon
Boudoir, toilette, carriage, drawing-room, and ball-room,
Satin for worsted exchange, gros-de-naples for plain linsey-
      woolsey,
Sandals of silk for clogs, for health lackadaisical fancies!

So, feel women, not dolls; so feel the sap of existence
Circulate up through their roots from the far-away centre of all
    things,
Circulate up from the depths to the bud on the twig that is
    topmost!
Yes, we should see them delighted, delighted ourselves in the
    seeing,
Bending with blue cotton gown skirted-up over striped linsey-
    woolsey,
Milking the kine in the field, like Rachel, watering cattle,
Rachel, when at the well the predestined beheld and kissed her,
Or, with pail upon head, like Dora beloved of Alexis,
Comely, with well-poised pail over neck arching soft to the
    shoulders,
Comely in gracefullest act, one arm uplifted to stay it,
Home from the river or pump moving stately and calm to the
    laundry;
Ay, doing household work, as many sweet girls I have looked at,
Needful household work, which some one, after all, must do,
Needful, graceful therefore, as washing, cooking, and scouring,
Or, if you please, with the fork in the garden uprooting potatoes. —
    Or, — high-kilted perhaps, cried Lindsay, at last successful,
Lindsay, this long time swelling with scorn and pent-up fury,
Or high-kilted perhaps, as once at Dundee I saw them,
Petticoats up to the knees, or even, it might be, above them,
Matching their lily-white legs with the clothes that they trod in the
    wash-tub!
    Laughter ensued at this; and seeing the Tutor embarrassed,
It was from them, I suppose, said Arthur, smiling sedately,
Lindsay learnt the tune we all have learnt from Lindsay,
*For oh, he was a roguey, the Piper o' Dundee.*
    Laughter ensued again; and the Tutor, recovering slowly,
Said, Are not these perhaps as doubtful as other attractions?
There is a truth in your view, but I think extremely distorted;
Still there is a truth, I own, I understand you entirely.
    While the Tutor was gathering his purposes, Arthur continued,
Is not all this the same that one hears at common-room breakfasts,
Or perhaps Trinity wines, about Gothic buildings and Beauty?

And with a start from the sofa came Hobbes; with a cry from the
    sofa,
Where he was laid, the great Hobbes, contemplative, corpulent,
    witty,
Author forgotten and silent of currentest phrases and fancies,
Mute and exuberant by turns, a fountain at intervals playing,
Mute and abstracted, or strong and abundant as rain in the tropics;
Studious; careless of dress; inobservant; by smooth persuasions
Lately decoyed into kilt on example of Hope and the Piper,
Hope an Antinoüs mere, Hyperion of calves the Piper.

Beautiful! cried he upleaping, analogy perfect to madness!
O inexhaustible source of thought, shall I call it, or fancy!
Wonderful spring, at whose touch doors fly, what a vista disclosing!
Exquisite germ! Ah no, crude fingers shall not soil thee;
Rest, lovely pearl, in my brain, and slowly mature in the oyster.

While at the exquisite pearl they were laughing and corpulent
    oyster,
Ah, could they only be taught, he resumed, by a Pugin of women,
How even churning and washing, the dairy, the scullery duties,
Wait but a touch to redeem and convert them to charms and
    attractions,
Scrubbing requires for true grace but frank and artistical handling,
And the removal of slops to be ornamentally treated.

Philip who speaks like a book (retiring and pausing he added),
Philip here, who speaks — like a folio, say'st thou, Piper?
Philip shall write us a book, a Treatise upon *The Laws of
Architectural Beauty in Application to Women;*
Illustrations, of course, and a Parker's Glossary pendent,
Where shall in specimen seen be the sculliony stumpy-columnar,
(Which to a reverent taste is perhaps the most moving of any,)
Rising to grace of true woman in English the Early and Later,
Charming us still in fulfilling the Richer and Loftier stages,
Lost, ere we end, in the Lady-Debased and the Lady-Flamboyant:
Whence why in satire and spite too merciless onward pursue her
Hither to hideous close, Modern-Florid, modern-fine-lady?
No, I will leave it to you, my Philip, my Pugin of women.

Leave it to Arthur, said Adam, to think of, and not to play
    with.

You are young, you know, he said, resuming, to Philip,
You are young, he proceeded, with something of fervour to
     Hewson,
You are a boy; when you grow to a man you'll find things alter.
You will then seek only the good, will scorn the attractive,
Scorn all mere cosmetics, as now of rank and fashion,
Delicate hands, and wealth, so then of poverty also,
Poverty truly attractive, more truly, I bear you witness.
Good, wherever it's found, you will choose, be it humble or stately,
Happy if only you find, and finding do not lose it.
Yes, we must seek what is good, it always and it only;
Not indeed absolute good, good for us, as is said in the Ethics,
That which is good for ourselves, our proper selves, our best selves.
Ah, you have much to learn, we can't know all things at twenty.
Partly you rest on truth, old truth, the duty of Duty,
Partly on error, you long for equality.
                              Ay, cried the Piper,
That's what it is, that confounded *égalité*, French manufacture,
He is the same as the Chartist who spoke at a meeting in Ireland,
*What, and is not one man, fellow-men, as good as another?*
*Faith*, replied Pat, *and a deal better too!*
                              So rattled the Piper:
But undisturbed in his tenor, the Tutor.
                              Partly in error
Seeking equality, *is not one woman as good as another?*
I with the Irishman answer, *Yes, better too;* the poorer
Better full oft than richer, than loftier better the lower.
Irrespective of wealth and of poverty, pain and enjoyment,
Women all have their duties, the one as well as the other;
Are all duties alike? Do all alike fulfil them?
However noble the dream of equality, mark you, Philip,
Nowhere equality reigns in all the world of creation,
Star is not equal to star, nor blossom the same as blossom;
Herb is not equal to herb, any more than planet to planet.
There is a glory of daisies, a glory again of carnations;
Were the carnation wise, in gay parterre by greenhouse,
Should it decline to accept the nurture the gardener gives it,
Should it refuse to expand to sun and genial summer,

Simply because the field-daisy, that grows in the grass-plat beside it,
Cannot, for some cause or other, develope and be a carnation?
Would not the daisy itself petition its scrupulous neighbour?
Up, grow, bloom, and forget me; be beautiful even to proudness,
E'en for the sake of myself and other poor daisies like me.
Education and manners, accomplishments and refinements,
Waltz, peradventure, and polka, the knowledge of music and
            drawing,
All these things are Nature's, to Nature dear and precious.
We have all something to do, man, woman alike, I own it;
We have all something to do, and in my judgement should do it
In our station; not thinking about it, but not disregarding;
Holding it, not for enjoyment, but simply because we are in it.

     Ah! replied Philip, Alas! the noted phrase of the prayer-book,
*Doing our duty in that state of life to which God has called us,*
Seems to me always to mean, when the little rich boys say it,
Standing in velvet frock by mama's brocaded flounces,
Eying her gold-fastened book and the watch and chain at her
            bosom,
Seems to me always to mean, Eat, drink, and never mind others.

     Nay, replied Adam, smiling, so far your economy leads me,
Velvet and gold and brocade are nowise to my fancy.
Nay, he added, believe me, I like luxurious living
Even as little as you, and grieve in my soul not seldom,
More for the rich indeed than the poor, who are not so guilty.

     So the discussion closed; and, said Arthur, Now it is my turn,
How will my argument please you? To-morrow we start on our
            travel.
     And took up Hope the chorus.

                                        To-morrow we start on our travel.
Lo, the weather is golden, the weather-glass, say they, rising;
Four weeks here have we read; four weeks will we read hereafter;
Three weeks hence will return and think of classes and classics.
Fare ye well, meantime, forgotten, unnamed, undreamt of,
History, Science, and Poets! lo, deep in dustiest cupboard,
Thookydid, Oloros' son, Halimoosian, here lieth buried!
Slumber in Liddell-and-Scott, O musical chaff of old Athens,
Dishes, and fishes, bird, beast, and sesquipedalian blackguard!

Sleep, weary ghosts, be at peace and abode in your lexicon-limbo!
Sleep, as in lava for ages your Herculanean kindred,
Sleep, and for aught that I care, 'the sleep that knows no waking,'
Æschylus, Sophocles, Homer, Herodotus, Pindar, and Plato.
Three weeks hence be it time to exhume our dreary classics.

And in the chorus joined Lindsay, the Piper, the Dialectician.
Three weeks hence we return to the *shop* and the *wash-hand-stand-basin,*
(These are the Piper's names for the bathing-place and the cottage)
Three weeks hence unbury *Thicksides* and *hairy* Aldrich.

But the Tutor enquired, the grave man, nick-named Adam,
Who are they that go, and when do they promise returning?

And a silence ensued, and the Tutor himself continued,
Airlie remains, I presume, he continued, and Hobbes and Hewson.

Answer was made him by Philip, the poet, the eloquent
        speaker:
Airlie remains, I presume, was the answer, and Hobbes,
        peradventure;
Tarry let Airlie May-fairly, and Hobbes, brief-kilted hero,
Tarry let Hobbes in kilt, and Airlie 'abide in his breeches;'
Tarry let these, and read, four Pindars apiece an it like them!
Weary of reading am I, and weary of walks prescribed us;
Weary of Ethic and Logic, of Rhetoric yet more weary,
Eager to range over heather unfettered of gillie and marquis,
I will away with the rest, and bury my dismal classics.

And to the Tutor rejoining, Be mindful; you go up at Easter,
This was the answer returned by Philip, the Pugin of Women.
Good are the Ethics, I wis; good absolute, not for me, though;
Good, too, Logic, of course; in itself, but not in fine weather.
Three weeks hence, with the rain, to Prudence, Temperance,
        Justice,
Virtues Moral and Mental, with Latin prose included,
Three weeks hence we return, to cares of classes and classics.
I will away with the rest, and bury my dismal classics.

But the Tutor enquired, the grave man, nick-named Adam,
Where do you mean to go, and whom do you mean to visit?

And he was answered by Hope, the Viscount, His Honour, of
        Ilay.

Kitcat, a Trinity *coach*, has a party at Drumnadrochit,
Up on the side of Loch Ness, in the beautiful valley of Urquhart;
Mainwaring says they will lodge us, and feed us, and give us a lift
    too;
Only they talk ere long to remove to Glenmorison. Then at
Castleton, high in Braemar, strange home, with his earliest party,
Harrison, fresh from the schools, has James and Jones and Lauder.
Thirdly, a Cambridge man I know, Smith, a senior wrangler,
With a mathematical score hangs-out at Inverary.
    Finally, too, from the kilt and the sofa said Hobbes in
      conclusion,
Finally Philip must hunt for that home of the probable poacher,
Hid in the braes of Lochaber, the Bothie of *What-did-he-call-it*.
Hopeless of you and of us, of gillies and marquises hopeless,
Weary of Ethic and Logic, of Rhetoric yet more weary,
There shall he, smit by the charm of a lovely potato-uprooter,
Study the question of sex in the Bothie of *What-did-he-call-it*.


III

*Namque canebat uti –*[*]

So in the golden morning they parted and went to the westward.
And in the cottage with Airlie and Hobbes remained the Tutor;
Reading nine hours a day with the Tutor Hobbes and Airlie;
One between bathing and breakfast, and six before it was dinner,
(Breakfast at eight, at four, after bathing again, the dinner)
Finally, two after walking and tea, from nine to eleven.
Airlier and Adam at evening their quiet stroll together
Took on the terrace-road, with the western hills before them;
Hobbes, only rarely a third, now and then in the cottage remaining,
E'en after dinner, eupeptic, would rush yet again to his reading;
Other times, stung by the oestrum of some swift-working
    conception,
Ranged, tearing-on in his fury, an Io-cow, through the mountains,
Heedless of scenery, heedless of bogs, and of perspiration,
On the high peaks, unwitting, the hares and ptarmigan starting.

[*] Virgil, *Eclogues*, VI, l. 31.

And the three weeks past, the three weeks, three days over,
Neither letter had come, nor casual tidings any,
And the pupils grumbled, the Tutor became uneasy,
And in the golden weather they wondered, and watched to the
    westward.
  There is a stream, I name not its name, lest inquisitive tourist
Hunt it, and make it a lion, and get it at last into guide-books,
Springing far off from a loch unexplored in the folds of great
    mountains,
Falling two miles through rowan and stunted alder, enveloped
Then for four more in a forest of pine, where broad and ample
Spreads, to convey it, the glen with heathery slopes on both sides:
Broad and fair the stream, with occasional falls and narrows;
But, where the glen of its course approaches the vale of the river,
Met and blocked by a huge interposing mass of granite,
Scarce by a channel deep-cut, raging up, and raging onward,
Forces its flood through a passage so narrow a lady would step it.
There, across the great rocky wharves, a wooden bridge goes,
Carrying a path to the forest; below, three hundred yards, say,
Lower in level some twenty-five feet, through flats of shingle,
Stepping-stones and a cart-track cross in the open valley.
  But in the interval here the boiling, pent-up water
Frees itself by a final descent, attaining a bason,
Ten feet wide and eighteen long, with whiteness and fury
Occupied partly, but mostly pellucid, pure, a mirror;
Beautiful there for the colour derived from green rocks under;
Beautiful, most of all, where beads of foam uprising
Mingle their clouds of white with the delicate hue of the stillness.
Cliff over cliff for its sides, with rowan and pendent birch boughs,
Here it lies, unthought of above at the bridge and pathway,
Still more enclosed from below by wood and rocky projection.
You are shut in, left alone with yourself and perfection of water,
Hid on all sides, left alone with yourself and the goddess of bathing.
Here, the pride of the plunger, you stride the fall and clear it;
Here, the delight of the bather, you roll in beaded sparklings,
Here into pure green depth drop down from lofty ledges.
  Hither, a month agone, they had come, and discovered it;
    hither

(Long a design, but long unaccountably left unaccomplished,)
Leaving the well-known bridge and pathway above to the forest,
Turning below from the track of the carts over stone and shingle,
Piercing a wood, and skirting a narrow and natural causeway
Under the rocky wall that hedges the bed of the streamlet,
Rounded a craggy point, and saw on a sudden before them
Slabs of rock, and a tiny beach, and perfection of water,
Picture-like beauty, seclusion sublime, and the goddess of bathing.
There they bathed, of course, and Arthur, the Glory of headers,
Leapt from the ledges with Hope, he twenty feet, he thirty;
There, overbold, great Hobbes from a ten-foot height descended,
Prone, as a quadruped, prone with hands and feet protending;
There in the sparkling champagne, ecstatic, they shrieked and
        shouted.
'Hobbes's gutter' the Piper entitles the spot, profanely,
Hope 'the Glory' would have, after Arthur, the Glory of headers:
But, for before they departed, in shy and fugitive reflex
Here in the eddies and there did the splendour of Jupiter glimmer,
Adam adjudged it the name of Hesperus, star of the evening.
    Hither, to Hesperus, now, the star of evening above them,
Come in their lonelier walk the pupils twain and Tutor;
Turned from the track of the carts, and passing the stone and
        shingle,
Piercing the wood, and skirting the stream by the natural
        causeway,
Rounded the craggy point, and now at their ease looked up; and
Lo, on the rocky ledge, regardant, the Glory of headers,
Lo, on the beach, expecting the plunge, not cigarless, the Piper. —
    And they looked, and wondered, incredulous, looking yet once
        more.
Yes, it was he, on the ledge, bare-limbed, an Apollo, down-gazing
Eyeing one moment the beauty, the life, ere he flung himself in it,
Eyeing through eddying green waters the green-tinting floor
        underneath them,
Eyeing the bead on the surface, the bead, like a cloud, rising to it,
Drinking-in, deep in his soul, the beautiful hue and the clearness,
Arthur, the shapely, the brave, the unboasting, the Glory of
        headers;

Yes, and with fragrant weed, by his knapsack, spectator and critic,
Seated on slab by the margin, the Piper, the Cloud-compeller.
  Yes, they were come; were restored to the party, its grace and its
      gladness,
Yes, were here, as of old; the light-giving orb of the household,
Arthur, the shapely, the tranquil, the strength-and-contentment-
      diffusing,
In the pure presence of whom none could quarrel long, nor be
      pettish,
And, the gay fountain of mirth, their dearly beloved of Pipers.
Yes, they were come, were here: but Hewson and Hope — where
      they then?
Are they behind, travel-sore, or ahead, going straight, by the
      pathway?
  And from his seat and cigar spoke the Piper, the Cloud-
      compeller.
Hope with the uncle abideth for shooting. Ah me, were I with
      him!
Ah, good boy that I am, to have stuck to my word and my reading!
Good, good boy to be here, far away, who might be at Balloch!
Only one day to have stayed who might have been welcome for
      seven,
Seven whole days in castle and forest — gay in the mazy
Moving, imbibing the rosy, and pointing a gun at the horny!
  And the Tutor impatient, expectant, interrupted,
Hope with the uncle, and Hewson — with him? or where have
      you left him?
  And from his seat and cigar spoke the Piper, the Cloud-
      compeller.
Hope with the uncle, and Hewson — Why, Hewson we left in
      Rannoch,
By the lochside and the pines, in a farmer's house, — reflecting —
Helping to shear,* and dry clothes, and bring in peat from the
      peat-stack.
  And the Tutor's countenance fell, perplexed, dumb-foundered
Stood he, — slow and with pain disengaging jest from earnest.

* Reap (Clough's note).

He is not far from home, said Arthur from the water,
He will be with us to-morrow, at latest, or the next day.
    And he was even more reassured by the Piper's rejoinder.
Can he have come by the mail, and have got to the cottage before
        us?
    So to the cottage they went, and Philip was not at the cottage;
But by the mail was a letter from Hope, who himself was to follow.
    Two whole days and nights succeeding brought not Philip,
Two whole days and nights exhausted not question and story.
    For it was told, the Piper narrating, corrected of Arthur,
Often by word corrected, more often by smile and motion,
How they had been to Iona, to Staffa, to Skye, to Culloden,
Seen Loch Awe, Loch Tay, Loch Fyne, Loch Ness, Loch
        Arkaig,
Been up Ben-nevis, Ben-more, Ben-cruachan, Ben-muick-dhui;
How they had walked, and eaten, and drunken, and slept in
        kitchens,
Slept upon floors of kitchens, and tasted the real Glen-livat,
Walked up perpendicular hills, and also down them,
Hither and thither had been, and this and that had witnessed,
Left not a thing to be done, and had not a copper remaining.
    For it was told withal, he telling, and he correcting,
How in the race they had run, and beaten the gillies of Rannoch,
How in forbidden glens, in Mar and midmost Athol,
Philip insisting hotly, and Arthur and Hope compliant,
They had defied the keepers; the Piper alone protesting,
Liking the fun, it was plain, in his heart, but tender of game-law;
Yea, too, in Mealy glen, the heart of Lochiel's fair forest,
Where Scotch firs are darkest and amplest, and intermingle
Grandly with rowan and ash — in Mar you have no ashes,
There the pine is alone, or relieved by the birch and the alder —
How in Mealy glen, while stags were starting before, they
Made the watcher believe they were guests from Achnacarry.

    And there was told moreover, he telling, the other correcting,
Often by word, more often by mute significant motion,
Much of the Cambridge *coach* and his pupils at Inverary,
Huge barbarian pupils, Expanded in Infinite Series,

Firing-off signal guns (great scandal) from window to window,
(For they were lodging perforce in distant and numerous houses,)
Signals, when, one retiring, another should go to the Tutor: —
Much too of Kitcat, of course, and the party at Drumnadrocheit,
Mainwaring, Foley, and Fraser, their idleness horrid and dog-cart;
Drumnadrocheit was *seedy*, Glenmorison *adequate*, but at
Castleton, high in Braemar, were the *clippingest* places for bathing,
One by the bridge in the village, indecent, *the Town-Hall*
     christened,
Where had Lauder howbeit been bathing, and Harrison also,
Harrison even, the Tutor; another like Hesperus here, and
Up the water of Eye half-a-dozen at least, all *stunners*.
     And it was told, the Piper narrating and Arthur correcting.
Colouring he, dilating, magniloquent, glorying in picture,
He to a matter-of-fact still softening, paring, abating,
He to the great might-have-been upsoaring, sublime and ideal,
He to the merest it-was restricting, diminishing, dwarfing,
River to streamlet reducing, and fall to slope subduing,
So was it told, the Piper narrating, corrected of Arthur,
How under Linn of Dee, where over rocks, between rocks,
Freed from prison the river comes, pouring, rolling, rushing,
Then at a sudden descent goes sliding, gliding, unbroken,
Falling, sliding, gliding, in narrow space collected,
Save for a ripple at last, a sheeted descent unbroken, —
How to the element offering their bodies, downshooting the fall,
     they
Mingled themselves with the flood and the force of imperious
     water.
     And it was told too, Arthur narrating, the Piper correcting,
How, as one comes to the level, the weight of the downward
     impulse
Carries the head under water, delightful, unspeakable; how the
Piper, here ducked and blinded, got stray, and borne-off by the
     current
Wounded his lily-white thighs, below, at the craggy corner.
     And it was told, the Piper resuming, corrected of Arthur,
More by word than motion, change ominous, noted of Adam,
How at the floating-bridge of Laggan, one morning at sunrise,

63

Came, in default of the ferryman, out of her bed a brave lassie;
And, as Philip and she together were turning the handles,
Winding the chain by which the boat works over the water,
Hands intermingled with hands, and at last, as they stept from the
    boatie,
Turning about, they saw lips also mingle with lips; but
That was flatly denied and loudly exclaimed at by Arthur:
How at the General's hut, the Inn by the Foyers Fall, where
Over the loch looks at you the summit of Méalfourvónie,
How here too he was hunted at morning, and found in the kitchen
Watching the porridge being made, pronouncing them smoked
    for certain,
Watching the porridge being made, and asking the lassie that made
    them,
What was the Gaelic for *girl*, and what was the Gaelic for *pretty*;
How in confusion he shouldered his knapsack, yet blushingly
    stammered,
Waving a hand to the lassie, that blushingly bent o'er the porridge,
Something outlandish — *Slan*-something, *Slan leat*, he believed,
    *Caleg Looach*,
That was the Gaelic it seemed for 'I bid you good-bye, bonnie
    lassie;'
Arthur admitted it true, not of Philip, but of the Piper.
    And it was told by the Piper, while Arthur looked out at the
    window,
How in thunder and rain — it is wetter far to the westward, —
Thunder and rain and wind, losing heart and road, they were
    welcomed,
Welcomed, and three days detained at a farm by the lochside of
    Rannoch;
How in the three days' detention was Philip observed to be
    smitten,
Smitten by golden-haired Katie, the youngest and comeliest
    daughter;
Was he not seen, even Arthur observed it, from breakfast to
    bed-time,
Following her motions with eyes ever brightening, softening ever?
Did he not fume, fret, and fidget to find her stand waiting at table?

Was he not one mere St. Vitus' dance, when he saw her at nightfall
Go through the rain to fetch peat, through beating rain to the
            peat-stack?
How too a dance, as it happened, was given by Grant of
            Glenurchie,
And with the farmer they went as the farmer's guests to attend it;
Philip stayed dancing till daylight, — and evermore with Katie;
How the whole next afternoon he was with her away in the
            shearing,
And the next morning ensuing was found in the ingle beside her
Kneeling, picking the peats from her apron, — blowing together,
Both, between laughing, with lips distended, to kindle the embers;
Lips were so near to lips, one living cheek to another, —
Though, it was true, he was shy, very shy, — yet it wasn't in
            nature,
Wasn't in nature, the Piper averred, there shouldn't be kissing;
So when at noon they had packed up the things, and proposed to
            be starting,
Philip professed he was lame, would leave in the morning and
            follow;
Follow he did not; do burns, when you go up a glen, follow after?
Follow, he had not, nor left; do needles leave the loadstone?
Nay, they had turned after starting, and looked through the trees at
            the corner,
Lo, on the rocks by the lake there he was, the lassie beside him,
Lo, there he was, stooping by her, and helping with stones from the
            water
Safe in the wind to keep down the clothes she would spread for the
            drying.
There they had left him, and there, if Katie was there, was Philip,
There drying clothes, making fires, making love, getting on too by
            this time,
Though he was shy, so exceedingly shy

                              You may say so, said Arthur,
For the first time they had known with a peevish intonation, —
Did not the Piper himself flirt more in a single evening,
Namely, with Janet the elder, than Philip in all our sojourn?
Philip had stayed, it was true; the Piper was loth to depart too,

Harder his parting from Janet than e'en from the keeper at Balloch;
And it was certain that Philip was lame.
                                        Yes, in his excuses,
Answered the Piper, indeed! —
                            But tell me, said Hobbes, interposing,
Did you not say she was seen every day in her beauty and bedgown
Doing plain household work as washing, cooking, scouring?
How could he help but love her? nor lacked there perhaps the
        attraction
That, in a blue cotton print tucked up over striped linsey-woolsey,
Barefoot, barelegged, he beheld her, with arms bare up to the
        elbows,
Bending with fork in her hand in a garden uprooting potatoes?
Is not Katie as Rachel, and is not Philip a Jacob?
Truly Jacob, supplanting an hairy Highland Esau?
Shall he not, love-entertained, feed sheep for the Laban of
        Rannoch?
Patriarch happier he, the long servitude ended of wooing,
If when he wake in the morning he find not a Leah beside him!
    But the Tutor enquired, who had bit his lip to bleeding,
How far off is the place? who will guide me thither to-morrow?


    But by the mail, ere the morrow, came Hope, and brought new
        tidings;
Round by Rannoch had come, and Philip was not at Rannoch;
He had left that noon, an hour ago.
                                With the lassie? —
With her? the Piper exclaimed, Undoubtedly! By great Jingo!
And upon that he arose, slapping both his thighs like a hero,
Partly, for emphasis only, to mark his conviction, but also
Part, in delight at the fun, and the joy of eventful living.
    Hope couldn't tell him, of course, but thought it improbable
        wholly;
Janet, the Piper's friend, he had seen, and she didn't say so,
Though she asked a good deal about Philip, and where he was
        gone to:
One odd thing by the bye, he continued, befell me while with her;
Standing beside her, I saw a girl pass; I thought I had seen her,

Somewhat remarkable-looking, elsewhere; and asked what her
    name was;
Elspie Mackaye, was the answer, the daughter of David! she's
    stopping
Just above here, with her uncle. And David Mackaye, where lives
    he?
It's away west, she said, they call it Tober-na-vuolich.

IV–VI: *The girl Hope sees passing, Elspie Mackaye, is also briefly
glimpsed by Philip, who recognizes but cannot place her: her glance seems
to pity him for behaving, in his infatuation for Kate, as if he were amongst
'fairy-land creatures'. After this, Philip flies from Kate and, taking Adam's
sage advice that he will in so doing be 'less likely to run into error' goes
instead into the company of those 'in his station'. He is heard of next flirting
with the Lady Maria at Rannoch. Meanwhile, the pupils 'in the joy of
their life and glory of shooting-jackets Bathed and read and roamed'. When
Philip writes again, he has fallen under the Lady Maria's spell and become
a 'prophet-apostate' who acclaims God's dispensation in putting 'the labour
of hodmen' and of miners in the service of so lovely a creature's ideal beauty.
But he recovers his true self and, consigning the Lady Maria to 'the sphere
of mere ornament' comes at last, as earlier (I) her father bid him do, to
Tober-na-Vuolich where his romance with Elspie flourishes. Clough, in
Part VII, 'will confront the great peril, and speak with the mouth of the
lovers':*

VII

*Vesper adest, juvenes, consurgite; Vesper Olympo
Expectata diu vix tandem lumina tollit.**

For she confessed, as they sat in the dusk, and he saw not her
    blushes,
Elspie confessed at the sports long ago with her father she saw him,
When at the door the old man had told him the name of the bothie;
There after that at the dance; yet again at a dance in Rannoch —
And she was silent, confused. Confused much rather Philip
Buried his face in his hands, his face that with blood was bursting.

* Catullus, *Carmina*, lxii, l. 1.

Silent, confused, yet by pity she conquered her fear, and continued.
Katie is good and not silly; be comforted, Sir, about her;
Katie is good and not silly; tender, but not like many
Carrying off, and at once for fear of being seen, in the bosom
Locking-up as in a cupboard the pleasure that any man gives them,
Keeping it out of sight as a prize they need be ashamed of;
That is the way, I think, Sir, in England more than in Scotland;
No, she lives and takes pleasure in all, as in beautiful weather,
Sorry to lose it, but just as we would be to lose fine weather.
And she is strong to return to herself and feel undeserted.
Oh, she is strong, and not silly; she thinks no further about you;
She has had kerchiefs before from gentle, I know, as from simple.
Yes, she is good and not silly; yet were you wrong, Mr. Philip,
Wrong, for yourself perhaps more than for her.

But Philip replied not,
Raised not his eyes from the hands on his knees.

And Elspie continued.
That was what gave me much pain, when I met you that dance at
    Rannoch,
Dancing myself too with you, while Katie danced with Donald;
That was what gave me such pain; I thought it all a mistaking,
All a mere chance, you know, and accident, — not proper
    choosing, —
There were at least five or six — not there, no, that I don't say,
But in the country about, — you might just as well have been
    courting.
That was what gave me much pain, and (you won't remember
    that, though,)
Three days after, I met you, beside my uncle's, walking,
And I was wondering much, and hoped you wouldn't notice,
So as I passed I couldn't help looking. You didn't know me.
But I was glad, when I heard next day you were gone to the
    teacher.

And uplifting his face at last, with eyes dilated,
Large as great stars in mist, and dim, with dabbled lashes,
Philip, with new tears starting,

You think I do not remember,
Said, — suppose that I did not observe! Ah me, shall I tell you?

Elspie, it was your look that sent me away from Rannoch.
It was your glance, that, descending, an instant revelation,
Showed me where I was, and witherward going; recalled me,
Sent me, not to my books, but to wrestlings of thought in the
        mountains.
Yes, I have carried your glance within me undimmed, unaltered,
As a lost boat the compass some passing ship has lent her,
Many a weary mile on road, and hill, and moorland:
And you suppose, that I do not remember, I had not observed it!
O, did the sailor bewildered observe when they told him his
        bearings?
O, did he cast overboard, when they parted, the compass they
        gave him?
   And he continued more firmly, although with stronger emotion:
   Elspie, why should I speak it? you cannot believe it, and should
        not:
Why should I say that I love, which I all but said to another?
Yet should I dare, should I say, O Elspie, you only I love; you,
First and sole in my life that has been and surely that shall be;
Could — O, could you believe it, O Elspie, believe it and spurn
        not!
Is it — possible, — possible, Elspie?
                                   Well, — she answered,
And she was silent some time, and blushed all over, and answered
Quietly, after her fashion, still knitting, Maybe, I think of it,
Though I don't know that I did: and she paused again; but it may
        be,
Yes, — I don't know, Mr. Philip, — but only it feels to me
        strangely
Like to the high new bridge, they used to build at, below there,
Over the burn and glen on the road. You won't understand me.
But I keep saying in my mind — this long time slowly with
        trouble
I have been building myself, up, up, and toilfully raising,
Just like as if the bridge were to do it itself without masons,
Painfully getting myself upraised one stone on another,
All one side I mean; and now I see on the other
Just such another fabric uprising, better and stronger,

Close to me, coming to join me: and then I sometimes fancy, —
Sometimes I find myself dreaming at nights about arches and
        bridges, —
Sometimes I dream of a great invisible hand coming down, and
Dropping the great key-stone in the middle: there in my dreaming,
There I feel the great key-stone coming in, and through it
Feel the other part — all the other stones of the archway,
Joined into mine with a strange happy sense of completeness. But,
        dear me,
This is confusion and nonsense. I mix all the things I can think of.
And you won't understand, Mr. Philip.
                              But while she was speaking,
So it happened, a moment she paused from her work, and,
        pondering,
Laid her hand on her lap: Philip took it: she did not resist:
So he retained her fingers, the knitting being stopped. But emotion
Came all over her more and yet more, from his hand, from her
        heart, and
Most from the sweet idea and image her brain was renewing.
So he retained her hand, and, his tears down-dropping on it,
Trembling a long time, kissed it at last. And she ended.
And as she ended, uprose he; saying, What have I heard? Oh,
What have I done, that such words should be said to me? Oh, I
        see it,
See the great key-stone coming down from the heaven of heavens!
And he fell at her feet, and buried his face in her apron.

  But as under the moon and stars they went to the cottage,
Elspie sighed and said, Be patient, dear Mr. Philip,
Do not do anything hasty. It is all so soon, so sudden.
Do not say anything yet to any one.
                    Elspie, he answered,
Does not my friend go on Friday? I then shall see nothing of you:
Do not I go myself on Monday?
                  But oh, he said, Elspie;
Do as I bid you, my child; do not go on calling me Mr.;
Might I not just as well be calling you Miss Elspie?
Call me, this heavenly night, for once, for the first time, Philip.
  Philip, she said and laughed, and said she could not say it;

Philip, she said; he turned, and kissed the sweet lips as they said it.

But on the morrow Elspie kept out of the way of Philip;
And at the evening seat, when he took her hand by the alders,
Drew it back, saying, almost peevishly,
                                    No, Mr. Philip,
I was quite right, last night; it is too soon, too sudden.
What I told you before was foolish perhaps, was hasty.
When I think it over, I am shocked and terrified at it.
Not that at all I unsay it; that is, I know I said it,
And when I said it, felt it. But oh, we must wait, Mr. Philip!
We mustn't pull ourselves at the great key-stone of the centre;
Some one else up above must hold it, fit it, and fix it;
If we try ourselves, we shall only damage the archway,
Damage all our own work that we wrought, our painful
          upbuilding.
When, you remember, you took my hand last evening, talking,
I was all over a tremble: and as you pressed fingers
After, and afterwards kissed it, I could not speak. And then, too,
As we went home, you kissed me for saying your name. It was
          dreadful.
I have been kissed before, she added, blushing slightly,
I have been kissed more than once by Donald my cousin, and
          others;
It is the way of the lads, and I make up my mind not to mind it;
But, Mr. Philip, last night, and from you, it was different quite,
          Sir.
When I think of all that, I am shocked and terrified at it.
Yes, it is dreadful to me.
                              She paused, but quickly continued,
Smiling almost fiercely, continued, looking upward.
You are too strong, you see, Mr. Philip! just like the sea there,
Which *will* come, through the straits and all between the
          mountains,
Forcing its great strong tide into every nook and inlet,
Getting far in, up the quiet stream of sweet inland water,
Sucking it up, and stopping it, turning it, driving it backward,
Quite preventing its own quiet running: and then, soon after,

Back it goes off, leaving weeds on the shore, and wrack and
    uncleanness:
And the poor burn in the glen tries again its peaceful running,
But it is brackish and tainted, and all its banks in disorder.
That was what I dreamt all last night. I was the burnie,
Trying to get along through the tyrannous brine, and could not;
I was confined and squeezed in the coils of the great salt tide, that
Would mix-in itself with me, and change me; I felt myself
    changing;
And I struggled, and screamed, I believe, in my dream. It was
    dreadful.
You are too strong, Mr. Philip! I am but a poor slender burnie,
Used to the glens and the rocks, the rowan and birch of the
    woodies,
Quite unused to the great salt sea; quite afraid and unwilling.
  Ere she had spoken two words, had Philip released her fingers:
As she went on, he recoiled, fell back, and shook, and shivered;
There he stood, looking pale and ghastly; when she had ended,
Answering in hollow voice,
                      It is true; oh quite true, Elspie;
Oh, you are always right; oh, what, what have I been doing!
I will depart to-morrow. But oh, forget me not wholly,
Wholly, Elspie, nor hate me, no, do not hate me, my Elspie.
  But a revulsion passed through the brain and bosom of Elspie;
And she got up from her seat on the rock, putting by her
    knitting;
Went to him, where he stood, and answered:
                          No, Mr. Philip,
No, you are good, Mr. Philip, and gentle; and I am the foolish;
No, Mr. Philip, forgive me.
                    She stepped right to him, and boldly
Took up his hand, and placed it in hers; he daring no movement;
Took up the cold hanging hand, up-forcing the heavy elbow.
I am afraid, she said, but I will! and kissed the fingers.
And he fell on his knees and kissed her own past counting.

  But a revulsion wrought in the brain and bosom of Elspie;
And the passion she just had compared to the vehement ocean,

72

Urging in high spring-tide its masterful way through the
 mountains,
Forcing and flooding the silvery stream, as it runs from the inland;
That great power withdrawn, receding here and passive,
Felt she in myriad springs, her sources, far in the mountains,
Stirring, collecting, rising, upheaving, forth-outflowing,
Taking and joining, right welcome, that delicate rill in the valley,
Filling it, making it strong, and still descending, seeking,
With a blind forefeeling descending ever, and seeking,
With a delicious forefeeling, the great still sea before it;
There deep into it, far, to carry, and lose in its bosom,
Waters that still from their sources exhaustless are fain to be added.
 As he was kissing her fingers, and knelt on the ground before
 her,
Yielding backward she sank to her seat, and of what she was doing
Ignorant, bewildered, in sweet multitudinous vague emotion,
Stooping, knowing not what, put her lips to the hair on his
 forehead:
And Philip, raising himself, gently, for the first time, round her
Passing his arms, close, close, enfolded her, close to his bosom.
 As they went home by the moon, Forgive me, Philip, she
 whispered;
I have so many things to think of, all of a sudden;
I who had never once thought a thing, — in my ignorant
 Highlands.


VIII: *Elspie has misgivings about her fitness to marry Philip: should she
'herself be An inferior there where only equality can be?' (In 1848 few
would not have questioned her 'only') But the 'prudent' Adam sets her fears
at rest. Their betrothal receives her father's blessing — in any case he 'had
fancied the lad from the first' and has since found him both honest and useful
at sheep-shearing. Philip now returns to Oxford to work hard a year for his
degree, philosophize a little more constructively and then, as Clough's close
friend Thomas Arnold the Younger (upon whom Philip is partly modelled)
had done in 1847, sets sail for New Zealand ...*

## *Arva, beata Petamus arva!**

So on the morrow's morrow, with Term-time dread returning,
Philip returned to his books, and read, and remained at Oxford,
All the Christmas and Easter remained and read at Oxford.

Great was wonder in College when postman showed to butler
Letters addressed to David Mackaye, at Tober-na-vuolich,
Letter on letter, at least one a week, one every Sunday:

Great at that Highland post was wonder too and conjecture,
When the postman showed letters to wife, and wife to the lassies,
And the lassies declared they couldn't be really to David;
Yes, they could see inside a paper with E. upon it.

Great was surmise in College at breakfast, wine, and supper,
Keen the conjecture and joke; but Adam kept the secret,
Adam the secret kept, and Philip read like fury.

This is a letter written by Philip at Christmas to Adam.

There may be beings, perhaps, whose vocation it is to be idle,
Idle, sumptuous even, luxurious, if it must be:
Only let each man seek to be that for which nature meant him.
If you were meant to plough, Lord Marquis, out with you, and do
      it;
If you were meant to be idle, O beggar, behold, I will feed you.
If you were born for a groom, and you seem, by your dress, to
      believe so,
Do it like a man, Sir George, for pay, in a livery stable;
Yes, you may so release that slip of a boy at the corner,
Fingering books at the window, misdoubting the eighth
      commandment.
Ah, fair Lady Maria, God meant you to live, and be lovely;
Be so then, and I bless you. But ye, ye spurious ware, who
Might be plain women, and can be by no possibility better!
— Ye unhappy statuettes, and miserable trinkets,
Poor alabaster chimney-piece ornaments under glass cases,
Come, in God's name, come down! the very French clock by you
Puts you to shame with ticking; the fire-irons deride you.
You, young girl, who have had such advantages, learnt so quickly,

* Horace, *Epodes,* 16 ll. 41–2.

Can you not teach? O yes, and she likes Sunday school extremely,
Only it's soon in the morning. Away! if to teach be your calling,
It is no play, but a business: off! go teach and be paid for it.
Lady Sophia's so good to the sick, so firm and so gentle.
Is there a nobler sphere than of hospital nurse and matron?
Hast thou for cooking a turn, little Lady Clarissa? in with them,
In with your fingers! their beauty it spoils, but your own it
      enhances;
For it is beautiful only to do the thing we are meant for.
  This was the answer that came from the Tutor, the grave man,
      Adam.
When the armies are set in array, and the battle beginning,
Is it well that the soldier whose post is far to the leftward
Say, I will go to the right, it is there I shall do best service?
There is a great Field-Marshal, my friend, who arrays our
      battalions;
Let us to Providence trust, and abide and work in our stations.
  This was the final retort from the eager, impetuous Philip.
I am sorry to say your Providence puzzles me sadly;
Children of Circumstance are we to be? you answer, On no
      wise!
Where does Circumstance end, and Providence where begins it?
What are we to resist, and what are we to be friends with?
If there is battle, 'tis battle by night: I stand in the darkness,
Here in the mêlée of men, Ionian and Dorian on both sides,
Signal and password known; which is friend and which is
      foeman?
Is it a friend? I doubt, though he speak with the voice of a brother.
Still you are right, I suppose; you always are, and will be;
Though I mistrust the Field-Marshal, I bow to the duty of order.
Yet is my feeling rather to ask, where *is* the battle?
Yes, I could find in my heart to cry, notwithstanding my Elspie,
O that the armies indeed were arrayed! O joy of the onset!
Sound, thou Trumpet of God, come forth, Great Cause, to array
      us,
King and leader appear, thy soldiers sorrowing seek thee.
Would that the armies indeed were arrayed, O where is the battle!
Neither battle I see, nor arraying, nor King in Israel,

Only infinite jumble and mess and dislocation,
Backed by a solemn appeal, 'For God's sake do not stir, there !'
Yet you are right, I suppose; if you don't attack my conclusion,
Let us get on as we can, and do the thing we are fit for;
Every one for himself, and the common success for us all, and
Thankful, if not for our own, why then for the triumph of others,
Get along, each as we can, and do the thing we are meant for.
That isn't likely to be by sitting still, eating and drinking.

    These are fragments again without date addressed to Adam.

    As at return of tide the total weight of ocean,
Drawn by moon and sun from Labrador and Greenland,
Sets-in amain, in the open space betwixt Mull and Scarba,
Heaving, swelling, spreading, the might of the mighty Atlantic;
There into cranny and slit of the rocky, cavernous bottom
Settles down, and with dimples huge the smooth sea-surface
Eddies, coils, and whirls; by dangerous Corryvreckan:
So in my soul of souls through its cells and secret recesses,
Comes back, swelling and spreading, the old democratic fervour.

    But as the light of day enters some populous city,
Shaming away, ere it come, by the chilly day-streak signal,
High and low, the misusers of night, shaming out the gas lamps —
All the great empty streets are flooded with broadening clearness,
Which, withal, by inscrutable simultaneous access
Permeates far and pierces to the very cellars lying in
Narrow high back-lane, and court, and alley of alleys : —
He that goes forth to his walks, while speeding to the suburb,
Sees sights only peaceful and pure; as labourers settling
Slowly to work, in their limbs the lingering sweetness of slumber;
Humble market-carts, coming-in, bringing-in, not only
Flower, fruit, farm-store, but sounds and sights of the country
Dwelling yet on the sense of the dreamy drivers; soon after
Half-awake servant-maids unfastening drowsy shutters
Up at the windows, or down, letting-in the air by the doorway;
School-boys, school-girls soon, with slate, portfolio, satchel,
Hampered as they haste, those running, these other maidenly
       tripping;
Early clerk anon turning out to stroll, or it may be
Meet his sweetheart — waiting behind the garden gate there;

Merchant on his grass-plat haply, bare-headed; and now by this
   time
Little child bringing breakfast to 'father' that sits on the timber
There by the scaffolding; see, she waits for the can beside him;
Meantime above purer air untarnished of new-lit fires:
So that the whole great wicked artificial civilised fabric —
All its unfinished houses, lots for sale, and railway outworks —
Seems reaccepted, resumed to Primal Nature and Beauty: —
— Such — in me, and to me, and on me the love of Elspie!

   Philip returned to his books, but returned to his Highlands after;
Got a first, 'tis said; a winsome bride, 'tis certain.
There while courtship was ending, nor yet the wedding appointed,
Under her father he studied the handling of hoe and of hatchet:
Thither that summer succeeding came Adam and Arthur to see
   him
Down by the lochs from the distant Glenmorison; Adam the
   tutor,
Arthur, and Hope; and the Piper anon who was there for a visit;
He had been into the schools; plucked almost; all but a *gone-coon*;
So he declared never once had brushed up his *hairy* Aldrich;
Into the great might-have-been upsoaring sublime and ideal
Gave to historical questions a free poetical treatment;
Leaving vocabular ghosts undisturbed in their lexicon-limbo,
Took Aristophanes up at a shot; and the whole three last weeks
Went, in his life and the sunshine rejoicing, to Nuneham and
   Godstowe:
What were the claims of Degree to those of life and the sunshine?
There did the four find Philip, the poet, the speaker, the chartist,
Delving at Highland soil, and railing at Highland landlords,
Railing, but more, as it seemed, for the fun of the Piper's fury.
There saw they David and Elspie Mackaye, and the Piper was
   almost,
Almost deeply in love with Bella the sister of Elspie;
But the good Adam was heedful; they did not go too often.
There in the bright October, the gorgeous bright October,
When the brackens are changed, and heather blooms are faded,
And amid russet of heather and fern green trees are bonnie,
Alders are green, and oaks, the rowan scarlet and yellow,

Heavy the aspen, and heavy with jewels of gold the birch-tree,
There, when shearing had ended, and barley-stooks were garnered,
David gave Philip to wife his daughter, his darling Elspie;
Elspie the quiet, the brave, was wedded to Philip the poet.

So won Philip his bride. They are married and gone — But oh,
     Thou
Mighty one, Muse of great Epos, and Idyll the playful and tender,
Be it recounted in song, ere we part, and thou fly to thy Pindus,
(Pindus is it, O Muse, or Ætna, or even Ben-nevis?)
Be it recounted in song, O Muse of the Epos and Idyll,
Who gave what at the wedding, the gifts and fair gratulations.

Adam, the grave careful Adam, a medicine chest and tool-box,
Hope a saddle, and Arthur a plough, and the Piper a rifle,
Airlie a necklace for Elspie, and Hobbes a Family Bible,
Airlie a necklace, and Hobbes a Bible and iron bedstead.

What was the letter, O Muse, sent withal by the corpulent hero?
This is the letter of Hobbes the kilted and corpulent hero.

So the last speech and confession is made, O my eloquent
     speaker!
So *the good time is coming,*\* or come is it? O my chartist!
So the Cathedral is finished at last, O my Pugin of Women;
Finished, and now, is it true? to be taken out whole to New
     Zealand!
Well, go forth to thy field, to thy barley, with Ruth, O Boaz,
Ruth, who for thee hath deserted her people, her gods, her
     mountains.
Go, as in Ephrath of old, in the gate of Bethlehem said they,
Go, be the wife in thy house both Rachel and Leah unto thee!
Be thy wedding of silver, albeit of iron thy bedstead!
Yea, to the full golden fifty renewed be! and fair memoranda
Happily fill the fly-leaves duly left in the Family Bible.
Live, and when Hobbes is forgotten, may'st thou, an unroasted
     Grandsire,
See thy children's children, and Democracy upon New Zealand!
This was the letter of Hobbes, and this the postscript after.

---

\* 'The Good Time Coming'–Chartist Song, by Charles Mackay
(1814–1889).

Wit in the letter will prate, but wisdom speaks in a postscript;
Listen to wisdom — *Which things* — you perhaps didn't know, my
    dear fellow,
I have reflected; *Which things are an allegory*, Philip.
For this Rachel-and-Leah is marriage; which, I have seen it,
Lo, and have known it, is always, and must be, bigamy only,
Even in noblest kind a duality, compound, and complex,
One part heavenly-ideal, the other vulgar and earthy:
For this Rachel-and-Leah is marriage, and Laban their father
Circumstance, chance, the world, our uncle and hard taskmaster.
Rachel we found as we fled from the daughters of Heth by the
    desert;
Rachel we met at the well; we came, we saw, we kissed her;
Rachel we serve-for, long years, — that seem as a few days only,
E'en for the love we have to her, — and win her at last of Laban.
Is it not Rachel we take in our joy from the hand of her father?
Is it not Rachel we lead in the mystical veil from the altar?
Rachel we dream-of at night: in the morning, behold, it is Leah.
'Nay, it is custom,' saith Laban, the Leah indeed is the elder.
Happy and wise who consents to redouble his service to Laban,
So, fulfilling her week, he may add to the elder the younger,
Not repudiates Leah, but wins the Rachel unto her!
Neither hate thou thy Leah, my Jacob, she also is worthy;
So, many days shall thy Rachel have joy, and survive her sister;
Yea, and her children — *Which things are an allegory*, Philip,
Aye, and by Origen's head with a vengeance truly, a long one!
    This was a note from the Tutor, the grave man, nicknamed
        Adam.
I shall see you of course, my Philip, before your departure;
Joy be with you, my boy, with you and your beautiful Elspie.
Happy is he that found, and finding was not heedless;
Happy is he that found, and happy the friend that was with him.
    So won Philip his bride: —
                  They are married, and gone to New Zealand.
Five hundred pounds in pocket, with books, and two or three
    pictures,
Tool-box, plough, and the rest, they rounded the sphere to New
    Zealand.

There he hewed, and dug; subdued the earth and his spirit;
There he built him a home; there Elspie bare him his children,
David and Bella; perhaps ere this too an Elspie or Adam;
There hath he farmstead and land, and fields of corn and flax
    fields;
And the Antipodes too have a Bothie of Tober-na-vuolich.

*1848 (revised 1859–60)*

# From *Amours de Voyage*

*Oh you are sick of self-love, Malvolio,*
*And taste with a distempered appetite!*
SHAKESPEARE

*Il doutait de tout, même de l'amour.*
FRENCH NOVEL

*Solvitur ambulando*
   SOLUTIO SOPHISMATUM
    *Flevit amores* [*amorem*]
*Non elaboratum ad pedem.*
HORACE

## CANTO II

*Is it illusion? or does there a spirit from perfecter ages,*
  *Here, even yet, amid loss, change, and corruption abide?*
*Does there a spirit we know not, though seek, though we find, comprehend*
  *not,*
  *Here to entice and confuse, tempt and evade us, abide?*
*Lives in the exquisite grace of the column disjointed and single,*
  *Haunts the rude masses of brick garlanded gayly with vine,*
*E'en in the turret fantastic surviving that springs from the ruin,*
  *E'en in the people itself? is it illusion or not?*
*Is it illusion or not that attracteth the pilgrim transalpine,*
  *Brings him a dullard and dunce hither to pry and to stare?*
*Is it illusion or not that allures the barbarian stranger,*
  *Brings him with gold to the shrine, brings him in arms to the gate?*

## I. CLAUDE TO EUSTACE

What do the people say, and what does the government do? —
  you
Ask, and I know not at all. Yet fortune will favour your hopes;
  and
I, who avoided it all, am fated, it seems, to describe it.
I, who nor meddle nor make in politics, — I who sincerely
Put not my trust in leagues nor any suffrage by ballot,
Never predicted Parisian millenniums, never beheld a
New Jerusalem coming down dressed like a bride out of heaven
Right on the Place de la Concorde, — I, nevertheless, let me say it,
Could in my soul of souls, this day, with the Gaul at the gates, shed
One true tear for thee, thou poor little Roman Republic!
What, with the German restored, with Sicily safe to the Bourbon,
Not leave one poor corner for native Italian exertion?
France, it is foully done! and you, poor foolish England, —
You, who a twelvemonth ago said nations must choose for
  themselves, you
Could not, of course, interfere, — you, now, when a nation has
  chosen —
Pardon this folly! *The Times* will, of course, have announced the
  occasion,
Told you the news of to-day; and although it was slightly in error
When it proclaimed as a fact the Apollo was sold to a Yankee,
You may believe when it tells you the French are at Civita
  Vecchia.


## II. CLAUDE TO EUSTACE

*Dulce* it is, and *decorum*, no doubt, for the country to fall, — to
Offer one's blood an oblation to Freedom, and die for the Cause;
  yet
Still, individual culture is also something, and no man
Finds quite distinct the assurance that he of all others is called on,
Or would be justified, even, in taking away from the world that
Precious creature, himself. Nature sent him here to abide here,
Else why sent him at all? Nature wants him still, it is likely.
On the whole, we are meant to look after ourselves; it is certain

Each has to eat for himself, digest for himself, and in general
Care for his own dear life, and see to his own preservation;
Nature's intention, in most things uncertain, in this are decisive;
Which, on the whole, I conjecture the Romans will follow, and I
    shall.
  So we cling to our rocks like limpets; Oceans may bluster,
Over and under and round us; we open our shells to imbibe our
Nourishment, close them again, and are safe, fulfilling the purpose
Nature intended, — a wise one, of course, and a noble, we doubt
    not.
Sweet it may be and decorous, perhaps, for the country to die; but,
On the whole, we conclude the Romans won't do it, and I shan't.


### III. CLAUDE TO EUSTACE

Will they fight? They say so. And will the French? I can hardly,
Hardly think so; and yet — He is come, they say, to Palo,
He is passed from Monterone, at Santa Severa
He hath laid up his guns. But the Virgin, the Daughter of Roma,
She hath despised thee and laughed thee to scorn, — the Daughter
    of Tiber,
She hath shaken her head and built barricades against thee!
Will they fight? I believe it. Alas! 'tis ephemeral folly,
Vain and ephemeral folly, of course, compared with pictures,
Statues, and antique gems! — Indeed: and yet indeed too,
Yet, methought, in broad day did I dream, — tell it not in St.
    James's,
Whisper it not in thy courts, O Christ Church! — yet did I,
    waking,
Dream of a cadence that sings, *Si tombent nos jeunes héros, la*
*Terre en produit de nouveaux contre vous tous prêts à se battre;** 
Dreamt of great indignations and angers transcendental,
Dreamt of a sword at my side and a battle-horse underneath me.


### IV. CLAUDE TO EUSTACE

Now supposing the French or the Neapolitan soldier
Should by some evil chance come exploring the Maison Serny

          * From the 'Marseillaise'.

(Where the family English are all to assemble for safety),
Am I prepared to lay down my life for the British female?
Really, who knows? One has bowed and talked, till, little by little,
All the natural heat has escaped of the chivalrous spirit.
Oh, one conformed, of course; but one doesn't die for good
      manners,
Stab or shoot, or be shot, by way of a graceful attention.
No, if it should be at all, it should be on the barricades there;
Should I incarnadine ever this inky pacifical finger,
Sooner far should it be for this vapour of Italy's freedom,
Sooner far by the side of the d — d and dirty plebeians.
Ah, for a child in the street I could strike; for the full-blown lady —
Somehow, Eustace, alas! I have not felt the vocation.
Yet these people of course will expect, as of course, my protection,
Vernon in radiant arms stand forth for the lovely Georgina,
And to appear, I suppose, were but common civility. Yes, and
Truly I do not desire they should either be killed or offended.
Oh, and of course you will say, 'When the time comes, you will be
      ready.'
Ah, but before it comes, am I to presume it will be so?
What I cannot feel now, am I to suppose that I shall feel?
Am I not free to attend for the ripe and indubious instinct?
Am I forbidden to wait for the clear and lawful perception?
Is it the calling of man to surrender his knowledge and insight
For the mere venture of what may, perhaps, be the virtuous action?
Must we, walking our earth, discerning a little, and hoping
Some plain visible task shall yet for our hands be assigned us, —
Must we abandon the future for fear of omitting the present,
Quit our own fireside hopes at the alien call of a neighbour,
To the mere possible shadow of Deity offer the victim?
And is all this, my friend, but a weak and ignoble refining,
Wholly unworthy the head or the heart of Your Own
      Correspondent?


### V. CLAUDE TO EUSTACE

Yes, we are fighting at last, it appears. This morning as usual,
*Murray*, as usual, in hand, I enter the Caffè Nuovo;

Seating myself with a sense as it were of a change in the weather,
Not understanding, however, but thinking mostly of Murray,
And, for to-day is their day, of the Campidoglio Marbles,
*Caffè-latte!* I call to the waiter, — and *Non c' è latte,*
This is the answer he makes me, and this the sign of a battle.
So I sit; and truly they seem to think anyone else more
Worthy than me of attention. I wait for my milkless *nero,*
Free to observe undistracted all sorts and sizes of persons,
Blending civilian and soldier in strangest costume, coming in, and
Gulping in hottest haste, still standing, their coffee, —
    withdrawing
Eagerly, jangling a sword on the steps, or jogging a musket
Slung to the shoulder behind. They are fewer, moreover, than
    usual,
Much, and silenter far; and so I begin to imagine
Something is really afloat. Ere I leave, the Caffè is empty,
Empty too the streets, in all its length the Corso
Empty, and empty I see to my right and left the Condotti.

    Twelve o'clock, on the Pincian Hill, with lots of English,
Germans, Americans, French, — the Frenchmen, too, are
    protected, —
So we stand in the sun, but afraid of a probable shower;
So we stand and stare, and see, to the left of St. Peter's,
Smoke, from the cannon, white, — but that is at intervals only, —
Black, from a burning house, we suppose, by the Cavalleggieri;
And we believe we discern some lines of men descending
Down through the vineyard-slopes, and catch a bayonet gleaming.
Every ten minutes, however, — in this there is no misconception, —
Comes a great white puff from behind Michael Angelo's dome,
    and
After a space the report of a real big gun, — not the Frenchman's? —
That must be doing some work. And so we watch and conjecture.
    Shortly, an Englishman comes, who says he has been to St.
    Peter's,
Seen the Piazza and troops, but that is all he can tell us;
So we watch and sit, and, indeed, it begins to be tiresome. —
All this smoke is outside; when it has come to the inside,
It will be time, perhaps, to descend and retreat to our houses.

Half-past one, or two. The report of small arms frequent,
Sharp and savage indeed; that cannot all be for nothing:
So we watch and wonder; but guessing is tiresome, very.
Weary of wondering, watching, and guessing, and gossiping idly,
Down I go, and pass through the quiet streets with the knots of
National Guards patrolling, and flags hanging out at the windows,
English, American, Danish, — and, after offering to help an
Irish family moving *en masse* to the Maison Serny,
After endeavouring idly to minister balm to the trembling
Quinquagenarian fears of two lone British spinsters,
Go to make sure of my dinner before the enemy enter.
But by this there are signs of stragglers returning; and voices
Talk, though you don't believe it, of guns and prisoners taken;
And on the walls you read the first bulletin of the morning. —
This is all that I saw, and all I know of the battle.


VI. CLAUDE TO EUSTACE

Victory! Victory! — Yes! ah, yes, thou republican Zion,
Truly the kings of the earth are gathered and gone by together;
Doubtless they marvelled to witness such things, were astonished,
　　and so forth.
Victory! Victory! Victory! — Ah, but it is, believe me,
Easier, easier far, to intone the chant of the martyr
Than to indite any pæan of any victory. Death may
Sometimes be noble; but life, at the best, will appear an illusion.
While the great pain is upon us, it is great; when it is over,
Why, it is over. The smoke of the sacrifice rises to heaven,
Of a sweet savour, no doubt, to Somebody; but on the altar,
Lo, there is nothing remaining but ashes and dirt and ill odour.
　So it stands, you perceive; the labial muscles that swelled with
Vehement evolution of yesterday Marseillaises,
Articulations sublime of defiance and scorning, to-day col-
Lapse and languidly mumble, while men and women and papers
Scream and re-scream to each other the chorus of Victory. Well,
　　but
I am thankful they fought, and glad that the Frenchmen were
　　beaten.

85

So, I have seen a man killed! An experience that, among others!
Yes, I suppose I have; although I can hardly be certain,
And in a court of justice could never declare I had seen it.
But a man was killed, I am told, in a place where I saw
Something; a man was killed, I am told, and I saw something.

   I was returning home from St. Peter's; Murray, as usual,
Under my arm, I remember; had crossed the St. Angelo bridge;
    and
Moving towards the Condotti, had got to the first barricade, when
Gradually, thinking still of St. Peter's, I became conscious
Of a sensation of movement opposing me, — tendency this way
(Such as one fancies may be in a stream when the wave of the tide is
Coming and not yet come, — a sort of poise and retention);
So I turned, and, before I turned, caught sight of stragglers
Heading a crowd, it is plain, that is coming behind that corner.
Looking up, I see windows filled with heads; the Piazza,
Into which you remember the Ponte St. Angelo enters,
Since I passed, has thickened with curious groups; and now the
Crowd is coming, has turned, has crossed that last barricade, is
Here at my side. In the middle they drag at something. What is it?
Ha! bare swords in the air, held up! There seem to be voices
Pleading and hands putting back; official, perhaps; but the
    swords are
Many, and bare in the air. In the air? They descend; they are
    smiting,
Hewing, chopping — At what? In the air once more upstretched!
    And
Is it blood that's on them? Yes, certainly blood! Of whom, then?
Over whom is the cry of this furor of exultation?
   While they are skipping and screaming, and dancing their caps
    on the points of
Swords and bayonets, I do the outskirts back, and ask a
Mercantile-seeming bystander, 'What is it?' and he, looking
    always
That may, makes me answer, 'A Priest, who was trying to fly to
The Neapolitan army,' — and thus explains the proceeding.

You didn't see the dead man? No; — I began to be doubtful;
I was in black myself, and didn't know what mightn't happen —
But a National Guard close by me, outside of the hubbub,
Broke his sword with slashing a broad hat covered with dust, —
    and
Passing away from the place with Murray under my arm, and
Stooping, I saw through the legs of the people the legs of a body.
    You are the first, do you know, to whom I have mentioned the
    matter.
Whom should I tell it to, else? — these girls? — the Heavens
    forbid it! —
Quidnuncs at Monaldini's? — idlers upon the Pincian?
    If I rightly remember, it happened on that afternoon when
Word of the nearer approach of a new Neapolitan army
First was spread. I began to bethink me of Paris Septembers,
Thought I could fancy the look of the old 'Ninety-two. On that
    evening
Three or four, or, it may be, five, of these people were slaughtered.
Some declare they had, one of them, fired on a sentinel; others
Say they were only escaping; a Priest, it is currently stated,
Stabbed a National Guard on the very Piazza Colonna:
History, Rumour of Rumours, I leave it to thee to determine!
    But I am thankful to say the government seems to have strength to
Put it down; it has vanished, at least; the place is most peaceful.
Through the Trastevere walking last night, at nine of the clock, I
Found no sort of disorder; I crossed by the Island-bridges,
So by the narrow streets to the Ponte Rotto, and onwards
Thence by the Temple of Vesta, away to the great Coliseum,
Which at the full of the moon is an object worthy a visit.

### VIII. GEORGINA TREVELLYN TO LOUISA

Only think, dearest Louisa, what fearful scenes we have
    witnessed! —

        ☆      ☆      ☆

George has just seen Garibaldi, dressed up in a long white cloak,
    on
Horseback, riding by, with his mounted negro behind him:

This is a man, you know, who came from America with him,
Out of the woods, I suppose, and uses a *lasso* in fighting,
Which is, I don't quite know, but a sort of noose, I imagine ;
This he throws on the heads of the enemy's men in a battle,
Pulls them into his reach, and then most cruelly kills them :
Mary does not believe, but we heard it from an Italian.
Mary allows she was wrong about Mr. Claude *being selfish* :
He was *most* useful and kind on the terrible thirtieth of April.
Do not write here any more ; we are starting directly for Florence :
We should be off to-morrow, if only Papa could get horses ;
All have been seized everywhere for the use of this dreadful
    Mazzini.

P.S.

Mary has seen thus far. — I am really so angry, Louisa, —
Quite out of patience, my dearest ! What can the man be intending ?
I am quite tired ; and Mary, who might bring him to in a moment,
Lets him go on as he likes, and neither will help nor dismiss him.

## IX. CLAUDE TO EUSTACE

It is most curious to see what a power a few calm words (in
Merely a brief proclamation) appear to possess on the people.
Order is perfect, and peace ; the city is utterly tranquil ;
And one cannot conceive that this easy and *nonchalant* crowd, that
Flows like a quiet stream through street and market-place, entering
Shady recesses and bays of church, *osteria*, and *caffè*,
Could in a moment be changed to a flood as of molten lava,
Boil into deadly wrath and wild homicidal delusion.

Ah, 'tis an excellent race, — and even in old degradation,
Under a rule that enforces to flattery, lying, and cheating,
E'en under Pope and Priest, a nice and natural people.
Oh, could they but be allowed this chance of redemption ! — but
    clearly
That is not likely to be. Meantime, notwithstanding all journals,
Honour for once to the tongue and the pen of the eloquent writer !
Honour to speech ! and all honour to thee, thou noble Mazzini !

## X. CLAUDE TO EUSTACE

I am in love, meantime, you think; no doubt you would think so.
I am in love, you say; with those letters, of course, you would say so.
I am in love, you declare. I think not so; yet I grant you
It is a pleasure indeed to converse with this girl. Oh, rare gift,
Rare felicity, this! she can talk in a rational way, can
Speak upon subjects that really are matters of mind and of thinking,
Yet in perfection retain her simplicity; never, one moment,
Never, however you urge it, however you tempt her, consents to
Step from ideas and fancies and loving sensations to those vain
Conscious understandings that vex the minds of man-kind.
No, though she talk, it is music; her fingers desert not the keys; 'tis
Song, though you hear in the song the articulate vocables sounded,
Syllabled singly and sweetly the words of melodious meaning.
    I am in love, you say: I do not think so, exactly.


## XI. CLAUDE TO EUSTACE

There are two different kinds, I believe, of human attraction:
One which simply disturbs, unsettles, and makes you uneasy,
And another that poises, retains, and fixes and holds you.
I have no doubt, for myself, in giving my voice for the latter.
I do not wish to be moved, but growing where I was growing,
There more truly to grow, to live where as yet I had languished.
I do not like being moved: for the will is excited; and action
Is a most dangerous thing; I tremble for something factitious,
Some malpractice of heart and illegitimate process;
We are so prone to these things with our terrible notions of duty.


## XII. CLAUDE TO EUSTACE

Ah, let me look, let me watch, let me wait, unhurried, unprompted!
Bid me not venture on aught that could alter or end what is present!
Say not, Time flies, and Occasion, that never returns, is departing!
Drive me not out, ye ill angels with fiery swords, from my Eden,
Waiting, and watching, and looking! Let love be its own
        inspiration!
Shall not a voice, if a voice there must be, from the airs that environ,

89

Yea, from the conscious heavens, without our knowledge or effort,
Break into audible words? And love be its own inspiration?

Wherefore and how I am certain, I hardly can tell; but it *is* so.
She doesn't like me, Eustace; I think she never will like me.
Is it my fault, as it is my misfortune, my ways are not her ways?
Is it my fault, that my habits and modes are dissimilar wholly?
'Tis not her fault, 'tis her nature, her virtue, to misapprehend them:
'Tis not her fault, 'tis her beautiful nature, not ever to know me.
Hopeless it seems, — yet I cannot, though hopeless, determine to
       leave it:
She goes, — therefore I go; she moves, — I move, not to lose her.

Oh, 'tisn't manly, of course, 'tisn't manly, this method of wooing;
'Tisn't the way very likely to win. For the woman, they tell you,
Ever prefers the audacious, the wilful, the vehement hero;
She has no heart for the timid, the sensitive soul; and for
       knowledge, —
Knowledge, O ye Gods! — When did they appreciate knowledge?
Wherefore should they, either? I am sure I do not desire it.
   Ah, and I feel too, Eustace, she cares not a tittle about me!
(Care about me, indeed! and do I really expect it?)
But my manner offends; my ways are wholly repugnant;
Every word that I utter estranges, hurts, and repels her;
Every moment of bliss that I gain, in her exquisite presence,
Slowly, surely, withdraws her, removes her, and severs her from me.
Not that I care very much! — any way, I escape from the boy's own
Folly, to which I am prone, of loving where it is easy.
Not that I mind very much! Why should I? I am not in love, and
Am prepared, I think, if not by previous habit,
Yet in the spirit beforehand for this and all that is like it;
It is an easier matter for us contemplative creatures,
Us, upon whom the pressure of action is laid so lightly;
We, discontented indeed with things in particular, idle,
Sickly, complaining, by faith in the vision of things in general

Manage to hold on our way without, like others around us,
Seizing the nearest arm to comfort, help, and support us.
Yet, after all, my Eustace, I know but little about it,
All I can say for myself, for present alike and for past, is,
Mary Trevellyn, Eustace, is certainly worth your acquaintance.
You couldn't come, I suppose, as far as Florence to see her?

## XV. GEORGINA TREVELLYN TO LOUISA

... To-morrow we're starting for Florence,
Truly rejoiced, you may guess, to escape from republican terrors;
Mr. C. and Papa to escort us; we by *vettura*
Through Siena, and Georgy to follow and join us by Leghorn.
Then — Ah, what shall I say, my dearest? I tremble in thinking!
You will imagine my feelings, — the blending of hope and of
          sorrow!
How can I bear to abandon Papa and Mamma and my Sisters?
Dearest Louisa, indeed it is very alarming; but trust me
Ever, whatever may change, to remain your loving Georgina.

### P.S. BY MARY TREVELLYN

... 'Do I like Mr. Claude any better?'
I am to tell you, — and, 'Pray, is it Susan or I that attract him?'
This he never has told, but Georgina could certainly ask him.
All I can say for myself is, alas! that he rather repels me.
There! I think him agreeable, but also a little repulsive.
So be content, dear Louisa; for one satisfactory marriage
Surely will do in one year for the family you would establish;
Neither Susan nor I shall afford you the joy of a second.

### P.S. BY GEORGINA TREVELLYN

Mr. Claude, you must know, is behaving a little bit better;
He and Papa are great friends; but he really is too *shilly-shally*, —
So unlike George! Yet I hope that the matter is going on fairly.
I shall, however, get George, before he goes, to say something.
Dearest Louise, how delightful to bring young people together!

---

*Is it to Florence we follow, or are we to tarry yet longer,*
  *E'en amid clamour of arms, here in the city of old,*
*Seeking from clamour of arms in the Past and the Arts to be hidden,*
  *Vainly 'mid Arts and the Past seeking one life to forget?*
*Ah, fair shadow, scarce seen, go forth! for anon he shall follow, —*
  *He that beheld thee, anon, whither thou leadest, must go!*
*Go, and the wise, loving Muse, she also will follow and find thee!*
  *She, should she linger in Rome, were not dissevered from thee!*


## CANTO III, LETTERS VI–XI

### VI. CLAUDE TO EUSTACE

Juxtaposition, in fine; and what is juxtaposition?
Look you, we travel along in the railway-carriage, or steamer,
And, *pour passer le temps*, till the tedious journey be ended,
Lay aside paper or book, to talk with the girl that is next one;
And, *pour passer le temps*, with the terminus all but in prospect,
Talk of eternal ties and marriages made in heaven.

  Ah, did we really accept with a perfect heart the illusion!
Ah, did we really believe that the Present indeed is the Only!
Or through all transmutation, all shock and convulsion of passion,
Feel we could carry undimmed, unextinguished, the light of our
      knowledge!
  But for his funeral train which the bridegroom sees in the
      distance,
Would he so joyfully, think you, fall in with the marriage-
      procession?
But for that final discharge, would he dare to enlist in that service?
But for that certain release, ever sign to that perilous contract?
But for that exit secure, ever bend to that treacherous doorway? —
Ah, but the bride, meantime, — do you think she sees it as he
      does?
  But for the steady fore-sense of a freer and larger existence,
Think you that man could consent to be circumscribed here into
      action?
But for assurance within of a limitless ocean divine, o'er

Whose great tranquil depths unconscious the wind-tost surface
Breaks into ripples of trouble that come and change and endure
    not, —
But that in this, of a truth, we have our being, and know it,
Think you we men could submit to live and move as we do here?
Ah, but the women, — God bless them! they don't think at all
    about it.

    Yet we must eat and drink, as you say. And as limited beings
Scarcely can hope to attain upon earth to an Actual Abstract,
Leaving to God contemplation, to His hands knowledge confiding,
Sure that in us if it perish, in Him it abideth and dies not,
Let us in His sight accomplish our petty particular doings, —
Yes, and contented sit down to the victual that He has provided.
Allah is great, no doubt, and Juxtaposition his prophet.
Ah, but the women, alas! they don't look at it in that way.

    Juxtaposition is great; — but, my friend, I fear me, the maiden
Hardly would thank or acknowledge the lover that sought to
    obtain her,
Not as the thing he would wish, but the thing he must even put up
    with, —
Hardly would tender her hand to the wooer that candidly told her
That she is but for a space, and *ad-interim* solace and pleasure, —
That in the end she shall yield to a perfect and absolute something,
Which I then for myself shall behold, and not another, —
Which, amid fondest endearments, meantime I forget not, forsake
    not.
Ah, ye feminine souls, so loving and so exacting,
Since we cannot escape, must we even submit to deceive you?
Since so cruel is truth, sincerity shocks and revolts you,
Will you have us your slaves to lie to you, flatter and — leave you?


VII. CLAUDE TO EUSTACE

Juxtaposition is great, — but, you tell me, affinity greater.
Ah, my friend, there are many affinities, greater and lesser,
Stronger and weaker; and each, by the favour of juxtaposition,
Potent, efficient, in force, — for a time; but none, let me tell you,
Save by the law of the land and the ruinous force of the will, ah,

None, I fear me, at last quite sure to be final and perfect.
Lo, as I pace in the street, from the peasant-girl to the princess,
*Homo sum, nihil humani a me alienum puto, —*
*Vir sum, nihil fæminei,* — and e'en to the uttermost circle,
All that is Nature's is I, and I all things that are Nature's.
Yes, as I walk, I behold, in a luminous, large intuition,
That I can be and become anything that I meet with or look at :
I am the ox in the dray, the ass with the garden-stuff panniers ;
I am the dog in the doorway, the kitten that plays in the window,
On sunny slab of the ruin the furtive and fugitive lizard,
Swallow above me that twitters, and fly that is buzzing about me ;
Yea, and detect, as I go, by a faint but a faithful assurance,
E'en from the stones of the street, as from rocks or trees of the forest,
Something of kindred, a common, though latent vitality, greet me ;
And, to escape from our strivings, mistakings, misgrowths, and
      perversions,
Fain could demand to return to that perfect and primitive silence,
Fain be enfolded and fixed, as of old, in their rigid embraces.


### VIII. CLAUDE TO EUSTACE

And as I walk on my way, I behold them consorting and coupling ;
Faithful it seemeth, and fond, very fond, very probably faithful ;
All as I go on my way, with a pleasure sincere and unmingled.
    Life is beautiful, Eustace, entrancing, enchanting to look at ;
As are the streets of a city we pace while the carriage is changing,
As is a chamber filled-in with harmonious, exquisite pictures,
Even so beautiful Earth ; and could we eliminate only
This vile hungering impulse, this demon within us of craving,
Life were beatitude, living a perfect divine satisfaction.


### IX. CLAUDE TO EUSTACE

*Mild monastic faces in quiet collegiate cloisters :*
So let me offer a single and celibatarian phrase, a
Tribute to those whom perhaps you do not believe I can honour.
But from the tumult escaping, 'tis pleasant, of drumming and
      shouting,
Hither, oblivious awhile, to withdraw, of the fact or the falsehood,

And amid placid regards and mildly courteous greetings
Yield to the calm and composure and gentle abstraction that reign
o'er
*Mild monastic faces in quiet collegiate cloisters.*
   Terrible word, Obligation! You should not, Eustace, you
      should not,
No, you should not have used it. But, oh, great Heavens, I repel it!
Oh, I cancel, reject, disavow, and repudiate wholly
Every debt in this kind, disclaim every claim, and dishonour,
Yea, my own heart's own writing, my soul's own signature! Ah,
   no!
I will be free in this; you shall not, none shall, bind me.
No, my friend, if you wish to be told, it was this above all things,
This that charmed me, ah, yes, even this, that she held me to
   nothing.
No, I could talk as I pleased; come close: fasten ties, as I fancied;
Bind and engage myself deep; — and lo, on the following morning
It was all e'en as before, like losings in games played for nothing.
Yes, when I came, with mean fears in my soul, with a semi-
      performance
At the first step breaking down in its pitiful rôle of evasion,
When to shuffle I came, to compromise, not meet, engagements,
Lo, with her calm eyes there she met me and knew nothing of it, —
Stood unexpecting, unconscious. *She* spoke not of obligations,
Knew not of debt, — ah, no, I believe you, for excellent reasons.


X. CLAUDE TO EUSTACE

*Hang* this thinking, at last! what good is it? oh, and what evil!
Oh, what mischief and pain! like a clock in a sick man's chamber,
Ticking and ticking, and still through each covert of slumber
      pursuing.
   What shall I do to thee, O thou Preserver of Men? Have
      compassion;
Be favourable, and hear! Take from me this regal knowledge;
Let me, contented and mute, with the beasts of the field, my
      brothers,
Tranquilly, happily lie, — and eat grass, like Nebuchadnezzar!

Tibur is beautiful, too, and the orchard slopes, and the Anio
Falling, falling yet, to the ancient lyrical cadence;
Tibur and Anio's tide; and cool from Lucretilis ever,
With the Digentian stream, and with the Bandusian fountain,
Folded in Sabine recesses, the valley and villa of Horace: —
So not seeing I sang; so seeing and listening say I,
Here as I sit by the stream, as I gaze at the cell of the Sibyl,
Here with Albunea's home and the grove of Tiburnus beside me;
Tivoli beautiful is, and musical, O Teverone,
Dashing from mountain to plain, thy parted impetuous waters!
Tivoli's waters and rocks; and fair under Monte Gennaro
(Haunt even yet, I must think, as I wander and gaze, of the
        shadows,
Faded and pale, yet immortal, of Faunus, the Nymphs, and the
        Graces),
Fair in itself, and yet fairer with human completing creations,
Folded in Sabine recesses the valley and villa of Horace: —
So not seeing I sang; so now — Nor seeing, nor hearing,
Neither by waterfall lulled, nor folded in sylvan embraces,
Neither by cell of the Sibyl, nor stepping the Monte Gennaro,
Seated on Anio's bank, nor sipping Bandusian waters,
But on Montorio's height, looking down on the tile-clad streets, the
Cupolas, crosses, and domes, the bushes and kitchen-gardens,
Which, by the grace of the Tiber, proclaim themselves Rome of
        the Romans, —
But on Montorio's height, looking forth to the vapoury mountains,
Cheating the prisoner Hope with illusions of vision and fancy, —
But on Montorio's height, with these weary soldiers by me,
Waiting till Oudinot enter, to reinstate Pope and Tourist.
                              *Written mainly 1849; published 1858*

# THE SHORTER POEMS (II)

## *Bethesda. A Sequel**

I saw again the spirits on a day,
Where on the earth in mournful case they lay;
Five porches were there, and a pool, and round,
Huddling in blankets, strewn upon the ground,
Tied-up and bandaged, weary, sore and spent,
The maimed and halt, diseased and impotent.
For a great angel came, 'twas said, and stirred
The pool at certain seasons, and the word
Was, with this people of the sick, that they
Who in the waters here their limbs should lay
Before the motion on the surface ceased
Should of their torment straightway be released.

So with shrunk bodies and with heads down-dropt,
Stretched on the steps, and at the pillars propt,
Watching by day and listening through the night,
They filled the place, a miserable sight.

And I beheld that on the stony floor
He too, that spoke of duty once before,
No otherwise than others here to-day
Foredone and sick and sadly muttering lay.
'I know not, I will do — what is it I would say?
'What was that word which once sufficed alone for all,
'Which now I seek in vain, and never can recall?'
'I know not, I will do the work the world requires
'Asking no reason why, but serving its desire;

* To *The Questioning Spirit* (p. 29).

'Will do for daily bread, for wealth, respect, good name,
'The business of the day — alas, is that the same?'
And then, as weary of in vain renewing
His question, thus his mournful thought pursuing,
'I know not, I must do as other men are doing.'

But what the waters of that pool might be,
Of Lethe were they, or Philosophy;
And whether he, long waiting, did attain
Deliverance from the burden of his pain
There with the rest; or whether, yet before,
Some more diviner stranger passed the door
With his small company into that sad place,
And breathing hope into the sick man's face,
Bade him take up his bed, and rise and go,
What the end were, and whether it were so,
Further than this I saw not, neither know.

## Epi-Strauss-ium*

Matthew and Mark and Luke and holy John
Evanished all and gone!
Yea, he that erst, his dusky curtains quitting,
Through Eastern pictured panes his level beams transmitting,
With gorgeous portraits blent,
On them his glories intercepted spent,
Southwestering now, through windows plainly glassed,
On the inside face his radiance keen hath cast,

* This title is a pun upon epithalamium ('wedding song'): 'Strauss'
refers to D. F. Strauss, whose revolutionary *Leben Jesu* (1835) treated
Christ as human and his life — in the Gospel narratives — as mytho-
logical. Psalm 19 is relevant to the imagery and theme: 'The heavens
declare the glory of God; and the firmament sheweth his handywork. . . .
In them hath he set a tabernacle for the sun, which is as a bridegroom
coming out of his chamber. . . . His going forth is, from the end of the
heaven, and his circuit unto the ends of it. . . .' Through Strauss,
Clough suggests, Christ, the 'bridegroom' of the Church, is now more
clearly seen.

And in the lustre lost, invisible and gone,
Are, say you, Matthew, Mark and Luke and holy John?
Lost, is it? lost, to be recovered never?
However,
The place of worship the meantime with light
Is, if less richly, more sincerely bright,
And in blue skies the Orb is manifest to sight.


## Easter Day

NAPLES, 1849

Through the great sinful streets of Naples as I past,
With fiercer heat than flamed above my head
My heart was hot within me; till at last
My brain was lightened, when my tongue had said

     Christ is not risen!

    Christ is not risen, no,
    He lies and moulders low;
      Christ is not risen.

What though the stone were rolled away, and though
    The grave found empty there! —
    If not there, then elsewhere;
If not where Joseph laid Him first, why then
    Where other men
Translaid Him after; in some humbler clay
    Long ere to-day
Corruption that sad perfect work hath done,
Which here she scarcely, lightly had begun.
    The foul engendered worm
Feeds on the flesh of the life-giving form
Of our most Holy and Anointed One.
    He is not risen, no,
    He lies and moulders low;
      Christ is not risen.

Ashes to ashes, dust to dust;
As of the unjust, also of the just —
        Christ is not risen.

What if the women, ere the dawn was grey,
Saw one or more great angels, as they say,
Angels, or Him himself? Yet neither there, nor then,
Nor afterward, nor elsewhere, nor at all,
Hath He appeared to Peter or the Ten,
Nor, save in thunderous terror, to blind Saul;
Save in an after-Gospel and late Creed
        He is not risen indeed,
            Christ is not risen.

Or what if e'en, as runs the tale, the Ten
Saw, heard, and touched, again and yet again?
What if at Emmaüs' inn and by Capernaum's lake
        Came One the bread that brake,
Came One that spake as never mortal spake,
And with them ate and drank and stood and walked
        about?
        Ah! 'some' did well to 'doubt'!
Ah! the true Christ, while these things came to pass,
Nor heard, nor spake, nor walked, nor dreamt, alas!
        He was not risen, no,
        He lay and mouldered low,
            Christ was not risen.

As circulates in some great city crowd
A rumour changeful, vague, importunate, and loud,
From no determined centre, or of fact,
        Or authorship exact,
        Which no man can deny
        Nor verify;

        So spread the wondrous fame;
            He all the same
        Lay senseless, mouldering, low.
        He was not risen, no,
            Christ was not risen!

100

Ashes to ashes, dust to dust;
As of the unjust, also of the just —
    Yea, of that Just One too.
This is the one sad Gospel that is true,
        Christ is not risen.

---

Is He not risen, and shall we not rise?
    Oh, we unwise!
What did we dream, what wake we to discover?
Ye hills, fall on us, and ye mountains, cover!
    In darkness and great gloom
Come ere we thought it is *our* day of doom,
From the cursed world which is one tomb,
        Christ is not risen!

Eat, drink, and die, for we are men deceived,
Of all the creatures under heaven's wide cope
We are most hopeless who had once most hope
We are most wretched that had most believed.
        Christ is not risen.

Eat, drink, and play, and think that this is bliss!
    There is no Heaven but this!
    There is no Hell; —
Save Earth, which serves the purpose doubly well,
    Seeing it visits still
With equallest apportionments of ill
Both good and bad alike, and brings to one same dust
    The unjust and the just
    With Christ, who is not risen.

Eat, drink, and die, for we are souls bereaved,
Of all the creatures under this broad sky
We are most hopeless, that had hoped most high,
And most beliefless, that had most believed.
    Ashes to ashes, dust to dust;
    As of the unjust, also of the just —

Yea, of that Just One too.
It is the one sad Gospel that is true,
    Christ is not risen.

————————

Weep not beside the Tomb,
Ye women, unto whom
He was great solace while ye tended Him;
    Ye who with napkin o'er His head
And folds of linen round each wounded limb
    Laid out the Sacred Dead;
And thou that bar'st Him in thy Wondering Womb.
Yea, Daughters of Jerusalem, depart,
Bind up as best ye may your own sad bleeding heart;
Go to your homes, your living children tend,
    Your earthly spouses love;
    Set your affections *not* on things above,
Which moth and rust corrupt, which quickliest come to
        end:
Or pray, if pray ye must, and pray, if pray ye can,
For death; since dead is He whom ye deemed more than
        man,
    Who is not risen, no,
    But lies and moulders low,
        Who is not risen.

Ye men of Galilee!
Why stand ye looking up to heaven, where Him ye ne'er may
        see,
Neither ascending hence, nor hither returning again?
    Ye ignorant and idle fishermen!
Hence to your huts and boats and inland native shore,
    And catch not men, but fish;
    Whate'er things ye might wish,
Him neither here nor there ye e'er shall meet with more.
    Ye poor deluded youths, go home,
    Mend the old nets ye left to roam,

Tie the split oar, patch the torn sail;
It was indeed 'an idle tale',
 He was not risen.


And oh, good men of ages yet to be,
Who shall believe *because* ye did not see,
 Oh, be ye warned! be wise!
 No more with pleading eyes,
 And sobs of strong desire,
 Unto the empty vacant void aspire,
Seeking another and impossible birth
That is not of your own and only Mother Earth.
But if there is no other life for you,
Sit down and be content, since this must even do:
 He is not risen.


 One look, and then depart,
 Ye humble and ye holy men of heart!
And ye! ye ministers and stewards of a word
Which ye would preach, because another heard, —
 Ye worshippers of that ye do not know,
 Take these things hence and go;
 He is not risen.


Here on our Easter Day
We rise, we come, and lo! we find Him not;
Gardener nor other on the sacred spot,
Where they have laid Him is there none to say!
No sound, nor in, nor out; no word
Of where to seek the dead or meet the living Lord;
There is no glistering of an angel's wings,
There is no voice of heavenly clear behest:
 Let us go hence, and think upon these things
 In silence, which is best.
 Is He not risen? No —
 But lies and moulders low —
 Christ is not risen.

*(First published 1865)*

# The Latest Decalogue

Thou shalt have one God only; who
Would be at the expense of two?
No graven images may be
Worshipped, except the currency:
Swear not at all; for for thy curse
Thine enemy is none the worse:
At church on Sunday to attend
Will serve to keep the world thy friend:
Honour thy parents; that is, all
From whom advancement may befall:
Thou shalt not kill; but needst not strive
Officiously to keep alive:
Do not adultery commit;
Advantage rarely comes of it:*
Thou shalt not steal; an empty feat,
When it's so lucrative to cheat:
Bear not false witness; let the lie
Have time on its own wings to fly:
Thou shalt not covet; but tradition
Approves all forms of competition.†

* These MS. lines struck directly at the refined Victorian ideal of the 'pure woman' (the more 'animal' man could, regrettably, be expected to err):

> Adultery it is not fit
> Or safe, for women, to commit.

† These four lines were first printed from MS. in 1951, but they go beyond the scheme of the 'Decalogue':

> The sum of all is, thou shalt love,
> If any body, God above:
> At any rate shall never labour
> *More* than thyself to love thy neighbour.

## To the Great Metropolis

Traffic, to speak from knowledge but begun,
I saw, and travelling much, and fashion — Yea,
And if that Competition and Display
Make a great Capital, then thou art one,
One, it may be, unrivalled neath the sun.
But sovereign symbol of the Great and Good,
True Royalty, and genuine Statesmanhood,
Nobleness, Learning, Piety was none.
If such realities indeed there are
Working within unsignified, 'tis well;
The stranger's fancy of the thing thou art
Is rather truly of a huge Bazaar,
A railway terminus, a gay Hotel,
Anything but a mighty Nation's heart.

*(First published 1951)*

## Land of Empire*

O Land of Empire, art and love!
  What is it that you show me?
A sky for Gods to tread above,
  A soil for pigs below me!
O in all place and shape and kind
  Beyond all thought and thinking,

* An MS. copy was headed 'Resignation — to Faustus': evidently
this was a hit at Matthew Arnold's 'Resignation — to Fausta'.

The graceful with the gross combined,
    The stately with the stinking!
Whilst words of mighty love to trace,
    Which thy great walls I see on,
Thy porch I pace or take my place
    Within thee, great Pantheon,
What sights untold of contrast bold
    My ranging eyes must be on!
What though uprolled by young and old
    In slumbrous convolution
Neath pillared shade must lie displayed
    Bare limbs that scorn ablution,
Should husks that swine would never pick
    Bestrew that patterned paving,
And sores to make a surgeon sick
    For charity come craving?
Though oft the meditative cur
    Account it small intrusion
Through that great gate to quit the stir
    Of market-place confusion,
True brother of the bipeds there,
    If Nature's need requireth,
Lifts up his leg with tranquil air
    And tranquilly retireth:
Though priest think fit to stop and spit
    Beside the altar solemn,
Yet, boy, that nuisance why commit
    On this Corinthian column? —


O richly soiled and richly sunned,
Exuberant, fervid, and fecund!
    Are these the fixed condition
On which may Northern pilgrim come
To imbibe thine ether-air, and sum
    Thy store of old tradition?
Must we be chill, if clean, and stand
Foot-deep in dirt in classic land?

So is it: in all ages so,
And in all places man can know,
From homely roots unseen below
In forest-shade in woodland bower
The stem that bears the ethereal flower
Derives that emanative power;
From mixtures fetid foul and sour
Draws juices that those petals fill.

Ah Nature, if indeed thy will
Thou own'st it, it shall not be ill!
And truly here, in this quick clime
Where, scarcely bound by space or time,
The elements in half a day
Toss off with exquisitest play
What our cold seasons toil and grieve,
And never quite at last achieve;
Where processes, with pain and fear
Disgust and horror wrought, appear
The quick mutations of a dance,
Wherein retiring but to advance,
Life, in brief interpause of death,
One moment sitting, taking breath,
Forth comes again as glad as e'er
In some new figure full as fair,
Where what has scarcely ceased to be,
Instinct with newer birth we see —
What dies already, look you, lives;
In such a clime, who thinks, forgives;
Who sees, will understand; who knows,
In calm of knowledge find repose,
And thoughtful as of glory gone,
So too of more to come anon,
Of permanent existence sure,
Brief intermediate breaks endure.
    O Nature, if indeed thy will,
Thou ownest it, it is not ill!
And e'en as oft on heathy hill,

On moorland black, and ferny fells,
Beside thy brooks and in thy dells,
Was welcomed erst the kindly stain
Of thy true earth, e'en so again
With resignation fair and meet
The dirt and refuse of thy street
My philosophic foot shall greet,
So leave but perfect to my eye
Thy columns set against thy sky!

*Note*: ll. 1–34 remained unpublished until 1951, having been omitted by
the Victorian editors *pro pudore*.


## *Uranus**

When on the primal peaceful blank profound,
Which in its still unknowing silence holds
All knowledge, ever by withholding holds —
When on that void (like footfalls in far rooms),
In faint pulsations from the whitening East
Articulate voices first were felt to stir,
And the great child, in dreaming grown to man,
Losing his dream to piece it up began;
Then Plato in me said,
' 'Tis but the figured ceiling overhead,
With cunning diagrams bestarred, that shine
In all the three dimensions, are endowed
With motion too by skill mechanical,
That thou in height, and depth, and breadth, and power,
Schooled unto pure Mathesis, might proceed

* The title refers to the heavens (Greek: οὐρανός), not the planet. In
earlier texts this note was supplied: 'This thought is taken from a passage
on astronomy in Plato's *Republic*, . . . vii.529.D. "We must use the
fretwork of the sky as patterns, with a view to the study which aims at these
higher realities, just as if we chanced to meet with diagrams cunningly
drawn and devised by Dædalus or some other craftsman or painter".'

To higher entities, whereof in us
Copies are seen, existent they themselves
In the sole Kingdom of the Mind and God.
Mind not the stars, mind thou thy Mind and God.'
By that supremer Word
O'ermastered, deafly heard
Were hauntings dim of old astrologies;
Chaldean mumblings vast, with gossip light
From modern ologistic fancyings mixed,
Of suns and stars, by hypothetic men
Of other frame than ours inhabited,
Of lunar seas and lunar craters huge.
And was there atmosphere, or was there not?
And without oxygen could life subsist?
And was the world originally mist? —
Talk they as talk they list,
I, in that ampler voice,
Unheeding, did rejoice.


## To Spend Uncounted Years

To spend uncounted years of pain,
Again, again, and yet again,
In working out in heart and brain
    The problem of our being here;
To gather facts from far and near,
Upon the mind to hold them clear,
And, knowing more may yet appear,
Unto one's latest breath to fear
The premature result to draw —
Is this the object, end and law,
    And purpose of our being here?

## It Fortifies My Soul

It fortifies my soul to know
That, though I perish, Truth is so:
That, howsoe'er I stray and range,
Whate'er I do, Thou dost not change.
I steadier step when I recall
That, if I slip, Thou dost not fall.

## 'Say Not the Struggle Nought Availeth'

Say not the struggle nought availeth
    The labour and the wounds are vain,
The enemy faints not, nor faileth,
    And as things have been, things remain.

If hopes were dupes, fears may be liars;
    It may be, in yon smoke concealed,
Your comrades chase e'en now the fliers,
    And, but for you, possess the field.

For while the tired waves, vainly breaking,
    Seem here no painful inch to gain,
Far back through creeks and inlets making
    [Comes],* silent, flooding in, the main,

And not by eastern windows only,
    When daylight comes, comes in the light,
In front the sun climbs slow, how slowly,
    But westward, look, the land is bright.

* This seems the logical reading, though 'came' is usually printed.
(Compare Clough's stronger use of similar imagery in *The Bothie, IX*)

# Come Back, Come Back

Come back, come back, behold with straining mast
And swelling sail, behold her steaming fast;
With one new sun to see her voyage o'er,
With morning light to touch her native shore.
    Come back, come back.

Come back, come back, while westward labouring by,
With sail-less yards, a bare black hulk we fly,
See how the gale we fight with, sweeps her back,
To our last home, on our forsaken track.
    Come back, come back.

Come back, come back, across the flying foam
We hear faint far-off voices call us home,
Come back, ye seem to say; ye seek in vain;
We went, we sought, and homeward turned again.
    Come back, come back.

Come back, come back; and whither back or why?
To fan quenched hopes, forsaken schemes to try;
Walk the old fields; pace the familiar street;
Dream with the idlers, with the base compete.
    Come back, come back.

Come back, come back; and whither and for what?
To finger idly some old Gordian knot,
Unskilled to sunder, and too weak to cleave,
And with much toil attain to half-believe.
    Come back, come back.

Come back, come back; yea back, indeed, do go
Sighs panting thick, and tears that want to flow;
Fond fluttering hopes upraise their useless wings,
And wishes idly struggle in the strings;
    Come back, come back.

Come back, come back, more eager than the breeze,
The flying fancies sweep across the seas,
And lighter far than ocean's flying foam
The heart's fond message hurries to its home.
    Come back, come back!

Come back, come back!
Back flies the foam; the hoisted flag streams back;
The long smoke wavers on the homeward track,
Back fly with winds things which the winds obey,
The strong ship follows its appointed way.


## Were You With Me

Were you with me, or I with you,
There's nought, methinks, I might not do;
Could venture here, and venture there,
And never fear, nor ever care.

To things before, and things behind,
Could turn my thoughts, and turn my mind,
On this and that, day after day,
Could dare to throw myself away.

Secure, when all was o'er, to find
My proper thought, my perfect mind,
And unimpaired receive anew
My own and better self in you.


## O Qui Me

Amid these crowded pews must I sit and seem to pray,
All the blessed Sunday morning while I wish to be away,
While in the fields I long to be or on the hill-tops high,
The air of heaven about me, above, the sacred sky?

Why stay and form my features to a 'foolish face of' prayer,
Play postures with the body, while the Spirit is not there?
Not there, but wandering off to woods, or pining to adore
Where mountains rise or where the waves are breaking on the shore.

In a calm sabbatic chamber when I could sit alone,
And feed upon pure thoughts to work-day hours unknown,
Amidst a crowd of lookers-on why come, and sham to pray,
While the blessed Sunday morning wastes uselessly away?

Upon the sacred morning that comes but once a week,
Where'er the Voice is speaking, there let me hear it speak;
Await it in the chamber, abroad to seek it roam,
The Worship of the heavens attend, the Services of home.

Pent-up in crowded pews am I really bound to stay,
And to edify my neighbours make a sad pretence to pray,
And where the Truth indeed speaks, neglect to hear it speak,
On the blessed Sunday morning that comes but once a week?

(First published 1951)

## A London Idyll

On grass, on gravel, in the sun,
 And now beneath the shade,
They went, in pleasant Kensington
 A footman and a maid;
That Sunday morning's April glow
 How should it not impart
A stir about the veins that flow
 To feed the youthful heart?

  Ah years may come and years may bring
   The truth that is not bliss
  But will they bring another thing
   That can compare with this?

H              113              C.C.V.

I read it in that arm she lays
    So soft on his; her mien
Her step, her very gown betrays
    (What in her eyes were seen)
That not in vain the young buds round
    The cawing birds above
The airs, the incense of the ground
    Are whispering breathing love.


        Ah years may come, etc.


To inclination young and blind
    So perfect, as they lent,
By purest innocence confined,
    Unconscious free consent —
Pervasive Power of Vernal Change!
    On this thine earliest day
Canst thou have found in all thy range
    One fitter type than they?


        Ah years may come, etc.


Th' high-titled cares of adult strife,
    Which we our duties call,
Trades, arts, and politics of life,
    Say, have they after all
One other object end or use
    Than that, for girl and boy,
The punctual earth may still produce
    This golden flower of joy?


        Ah years may come, etc.


O odours of new-budding rose,
    O lily's chaste perfume,
O fragrance, that didst first unclose
    The young Creation's bloom! —

114

Ye hung around me, while in sun
　　Anon and now in shade
I watched in pleasant Kensington
　　The footman and the maid.

　　And years may come and years may bring
　　　　The truth that is not bliss
　　But will they bring another thing
　　　　That can compare with this?


# Two Translations

### I: From Catullus (*A Fragment*)

Live my Lesbia, live we ah and love we.
All this talk of the moralizing old folk
Set we down at the value of a penny
Suns may sink and arise again tomorrow
We when once is the little light departed
Have one night of sleep, without a waking
Sleep one sleep of a night without a dawning.


### II: From Goethe (*Über allen Gipfeln*)

Over every hill
　　All is still;
In no leaf of any tree
　　Can you see
The motion of a breath.
Every bird has ceased its song,
　　Wait; and thou too, ere long,
　　Shall be quiet in death.

# 'But That from Slow Dissolving Pomps of Dawn'

But that from slow dissolving pomps of dawn
No verity of slowly strengthening light
Early or late hath issued; that the day
Scarce-shown, relapses rather, self-withdrawn,
Back to the glooms of ante-natal night,
For this, O human beings, mourn we may.

# From *Dipsychus*

## PROLOGUE

'I hope it is in good plain verse', said my uncle; 'none of your hurry-scurry anapæsts, as you call them, in lines which sober people are reading for plain heroics. Nothing is more disagreeable than to say a line over two, or, it may be, three or four times, and at last not be sure that there are not three or four ways of reading, each as good and as much intended as another. *Simplex duntaxat et unum.* But you young people think Horace and your uncles old fools.'

'Certainly, my dear sir,' said I; 'that is, I mean, Horace and my uncle are perfectly right. Still, there is an instructed ear and an uninstructed. A rude taste for identical recurrences would exact sing-song from "Paradise Lost", and grumble because "Il Penseroso" doesn't run like a nursery rhyme.'

'Well, well,' said my uncle, '*sunt certi denique fines,* no doubt. So commence, my young Piso, while Aristarchus is tolerably wakeful, and do not waste by your logic the fund you will want for your poetry.'

## SCENE I

*Venice. The Piazza. Sunday, 9 p.m.*

*Dips.* The scene is different, and the place; the air
Tastes of the nearer North: the people too
Not perfect southern lightness. Wherefore then

Should those old verses come into my mind
I made last year at Naples?* O poor fool,
Still nesting on thyself!
'Through the great sinful streets of Naples as I past,
With fiercer heat than flamed above my head
My heart was hot within, the fire burnt, and at last
My brain was lightened when my tongue had said,
    Christ is not risen!'

*Spirit*     Christ is not risen? Oh indeed!
    Wasn't aware that was your creed.

*Dips.* So it goes on. Too lengthy to repeat —
    'Christ is not risen.'

*Spirit*                   Dear, how odd!
    He'll tell us next there is no God.
    I thought 'twas in the Bible plain,
    On the third day he rose again.

*Dips.* Ashes to Ashes, Dust to Dust;
    As of the Unjust also of the Just —
      Yea, of that Just One too!
    Is He not risen, and shall we not rise?
      O we unwise!

*Spirit*     H'm! and the tone then after all
    Something of the ironical?
    Sarcastic, say; or were it fitter
    To style it the religious bitter?

*Dips.*     Interpret it I cannot. I but wrote it —
    At Naples, truly, as the preface tells,
    Last year in the Toledo; it came on me,
    And did me good at once. At Naples then,
    At Venice now. Ah! and I think at Venice
    Christ is not risen either.

*Spirit*                 Nay —
    T'was well enough once in a way;

        * See 'Easter Day', p. 99.

Such things don't fall out every day.
Having once happened, as we know,
In Palestine so long ago,
How should it now at Venice here?
Where people, true enough, appear
To appreciate more and understand
Their ices, and their Austrian band,
And dark-eyed girls —

*Dips.*       The whole great square they fill,
From the red flaunting streamers on the staffs,
And that barbaric portal of St. Mark's,
To where, unnoticed, at the darker end,
I sit upon my step. One great gay crowd.
The Campanile to the silent stars
Goes up, above — its apex lost in air.
While these — do what?

*Spirit*                Enjoy the minute,
And the substantial blessings in it;
Ices, *par exemple*; evening air;
Company, and this handsome square;
Some pretty faces here and there;
Music! Up, up; it isn't fit
With beggars here on steps to sit.
Up — to the café! Take a chair
And join the wiser idlers there.
Aye! what a crowd! and what a noise!
With all these screaming half-breeched boys.
*Partout* dogs, boys, and women wander —
And see, a fellow singing yonder;
Singing, ye gods, and dancing too —
Tooraloo, tooraloo, tooraloo, loo;
Fiddle di, diddle di, diddle di da
*Figaro sù, Figaro giù* —
*Figaro quà, Figaro là!*
How he likes doing it! Ah, ha, ha!

*Dips.* While these do what — ah heaven!

*Spirit*                                    If you want to pray
            I'll step aside a little way.
            Eh? But I will not be far gone;
            You may be wanting me anon.
            Our lonely pious altitudes
            Are followed quick by prettier moods.
            Who knows not with what ease devotion
            Slips into earthlier emotion?

*Dips.*  While these do what? Ah, heaven, too true, at Venice
         Christ is not risen either!


### SCENE II — THE PUBLIC GARDEN

*Dips.*  Assuredly, a lively scene!
         And, ah, how pleasant, something green!
         With circling heavens one perfect rose
         Each smoother patch of water glows,
         Hence to where, o'er the full tide's face,
         We see the Palace and the Place,
         And the White dome. Beauteous but hot.
         Where in the meantime is the spot,
         My favourite, where by masses blue
         And white cloud-folds, I follow true
         The great Alps, rounding grandly o'er,
         Huge arc, to the Dalmatian shore?

*Spirit*    This rather stupid place to-day,
            It's true, is most extremely gay;
            And rightly — the Assunzione
            Was always a *gran' funzione*.

*Dips.*  What is this persecuting voice that haunts me?
         What? whence? of whom? How am I to detect?
         Myself or not myself? My own bad thoughts,
         Or some external agency at work,
         To lead me who knows whither?

*Spirit*                                    Eh?
            We're certainly in luck to-day:

119

What lots of boats before us plying —
Gay parties, singing, shouting, crying,
Saluting others past them flying!
What numbers at the landing lying!
What lots of pretty girls, too, hieing
Hither and thither — coming, going,
And with what satisfaction showing,
To our male eyes unveiled and bare
Their dark exuberance of hair,
Black eyes, rich tints, and sundry graces
Of classic pure Italian faces!

*Dips.* Off, off! Oh heaven, depart, depart, depart!
Oh me! the toad sly-sitting at Eve's ear
Whispered no dream more poisonous than this!

*Spirit* A perfect show of girls I see it is.
Ah, what a charming foot, ye deities!
In that attraction as one fancies
Italy's not so rich as France is;
In Paris —

*Dips.* Cease, cease, cease!
I will not hear this. Leave me!

*Spirit* So!
How do those pretty verses go?

*Ah comme je regrette*
*Mon bras si dodu,*
*Ma jambe bien faite*
*Et le temps perdu!*
*Et le temps perdu!**

'Tis here, I see, the custom too
For damsels eager to be lovered
To go about with arms uncovered;
And doubtless there's a special charm
In looking at a well-shaped arm.
In Paris, I was saying —

* The refrain of Béranger's *La Grand'mère*.

120

*Dips.*                            Ah me, me!
         Clear stars above, thou roseate westward sky,
         Take up my being into yours; assume
         My sense to own you only; steep my brain
         In your essential purity. Or, great Alps,
         That wrapping round your heads in solemn clouds
         Seem sternly to sweep past our vanities,
         Lead me with you — take me away; preserve me!
         — Ah, if it must be, look then, foolish eyes —
         Listen fond ears; but, oh, poor mind, stand fast!

*Spirit*     In Paris, at the Opera
             In the *coulisses* — but ah, aha!
             There was a glance, I saw you spy it —
             So! shall we follow suit and try it?
             Pooh! what a goose you are! quick, quick!
             This hesitation makes me sick.
             You simpleton! what's your alarm?
             She'd merely thank you for your arm.

*Dips.* Sweet thing! ah well! but yet I am not sure.
        Ah no. I think she did not mean it. No.

*Spirit*     Plainly, unless I much mistake,
             She likes a something in your make:
             She turned her head — another glance —
             She really gives you every chance.

*Dips.* Ah, pretty thing — well, well. Yet should I go?
        Alas, I cannot say. What should I do?

*Spirit*     What should you do? well, that is funny!
             I think you are supplied with money.

*Dips.* No, no — it may not be. I could, I would —
        And yet I would not — cannot. To what end?

*Spirit*     Trust her for teaching! Go but you,
             She'll quickly show you what to do.
             Well, well! It's too late now — they're gone;
             Some wiser youth is coming on.

                            121

*Dips.* O hateful, hateful, hateful! To the Hotel!

*Spirit* Pooh, what the devil! what's the harm?
  I merely bid you take her arm.

*Dips.* And I half yielded! O unthinking I!
  O weak weak fool! O God how quietly
  Out of our better into our worse selves
  Out of a true world which our reason knew
  Into a false world which our fancy makes
  We pass and never know — O weak weak fool.

*Spirit* Well, if you don't wish, why, you don't.
  Leave it! but that's just what you won't.
  Come now! how many times per diem.
  Are you not hankering to try 'em.

*Dips.* O moon and stars forgive! And thou, clear heaven,
  Look pureness back into me. O great God,
  Why, why in wisdom and in grace's name,
  And in the name of saints and saintly thoughts,
  Of mothers, and of sisters, and chaste wives,
  And angel woman-faces we have seen,
  And angel woman-spirits we have guessed,
  And innocent sweet children, and pure love,
  Why did I ever one brief moment's space
  To this insidious lewdness lend chaste ears,
  Or parley with this filthy Belial?

*Spirit* O were it that vile questioner that loves
  To thrust his fingers into right and wrong
  And before proof knows nothing — or the fear
  Of being behind the world — which is, the wicked.
  O yes, you dream of sin and shame —
  Trust me, it leaves one much the same.

---

* With the exception of Dipsychus' 'O moon and Stars forgive'
speech (which Mrs. Clough placed at the end of Scene II) this scene
remained in MS. until 1951.

'Tisn't Elysium any more
Than what comes after or before:
But heavens! as innocent a thing
As picking strawberries in spring.
You think I'm anxious to allure you —
My object is much more to cure you.
With the high amatory-poetic
My temper's no way sympathetic;
To play your pretty woman's fool
I hold but fit for boys from school
I know it's mainly your temptation
To think the thing a revelation,
A mystic mouthful that will give
Knowledge and death — none know and live!
I tell you plainly that it brings
Some ease; but the emptiness of things
(That one old sermon Earth still preaches
Until we practise what she teaches)
Is the sole lesson you'll learn by it —
Still you undoubtedly should try it.
'Try all things' — bad and good, no matter;
You can't till then hold fast the latter.
If not, this itch will stick and vex you
Your live long days till death unsex you —
Hide in your bones, for aught I know,
And with you to the next world go.
Briefly — you cannot rest, I'm certain,
Until your hand has drawn the curtain.
Once known the little lies behind it,
You'll go your way and never mind it.
Ill's only cure is, never doubt it,
To do — and think no more about it.


*Dips.*  Strange talk, strange words. Ah me, I cannot say.
Could I believe it even of us men
That once the young exuberance drawn off
The liquor would run clear; that once appeased
The vile inquisitive wish, brute appetite fed,

123

The very void that ebbing flood had left
From purer sources would be now refilled;
That to rank weeds of rainy spring mowed off
Would a green wholesome aftermath succeed
That the empty garnished tenement of the soul
Would not behold the seven replace the one:
Could I indeed as of some men I might
Think this of maidens alsoI But I know;
Not as the male is, is the female, Eve
Was moulded not as Adam.

Spirit                        Stuff!
         The women like it; that's enough.

Dips.   Could I believe, as of a man I might,
         So a good girl from weary workday hours
         And from the long monotony of toil
         Might safely purchase these wild intervals,
         And from that banquet rise refreshed, and wake
         And shake her locks and as before go forth
         Invigorated, unvitiate to the task
         But no it is not so.

Spirit                That may be true
         It is uncommon, though some do.
         In married life you sometimes find
         Proceedings something of the kind.

Dips.   No no, apart from pressure of the world
         And yearning sensibilities of soul,
         The swallowed dram entails the drunkard's curse
         Of burnings ever new; and the coy girl
         Turns to the flagrant woman of the street,
         Ogling for hirers, horrible to see.

Spirit      That is the high moral way of talking
         I'm well aware about street-walking

Dips.   Hungering but without appetite; athirst
         From impotence; no humblest feeling left
         Of all that once too rank exuberance.
         No kindly longing, no sly coyness now

Not e'en the elastic appetence of lust
Not a poor petal hanging to that stalk
Where thousands once were redolent and rich.
Look, she would fain allure; but she is cold
The ripe lips paled, the frolick pulses stilled,
The quick eye dead, the once fair flushing cheek
Flaccid under its paint; the once heaving bosom —
Ask not! — for oh, the sweet bloom of desire
In hot fruition's pawey fingers turns
To dullness and the deadly spreading spot
Of rottenness inevitably soon
That while we hold, we hate — Sweet Peace! no more!

*Spirit*    Fiddle di diddle, fal lal lal!
        By candlelight they are pas mal;
        Better and worse of course there are, —
        Star differs (with the price) from star.

*Dips.*  Could I believe that any child of Eve
        Were formed and fashioned, raised and reared for nought
        But to be swilled with animal delight
        And yield five minutes' pleasure to the male —
        Could I think cherry lips and chubby cheeks
        That seems to exist express for such fond play,
        Hold in suppression nought to come; o'ershell
        No lurking virtuality of more —

*Spirit*    It was a lover and his lass,
        With a hey and a ho, and a hey nonino!
        Betwixt the acres of the rye,
        With a hey and a ho, and a hey nonino!
        These pretty country folks would lie —
        In the spring time, the pretty spring time.

*Dips.*  And could I think I owed it not to her,
        In virtue of our manhood's stronger sight,
        Even against entreaty to forbear —

*Spirit*    O Joseph and Don Quixote! This
        A chivalry of chasteness is,

That turns to nothing all, that story
Has made out of your ancient glory!
Still I must urge, that though tis sad
Tis sure, once gone, for good or bad
The prize whose loss we are deploring
Is physically past restoring:
C'en est fait. Nor can God's own self
As Coleridge on the dusty shelf
Says in his wicked Omniana
Renew to Ina frail or Ana
The once rent hymenis membrana.
So that it needs consideration
By what more moral occupation
To support this vast population?

Dips.  Could I believe that purity were not
Lodged somewhere, precious pearl, e'en underneath
The hardest coarsest outside: could I think
That any heart in woman's bosom set
By tenderness o'ermastering mean desire,
Faithfulness, love, were unredeemable.
Or could I think it sufferable in me
For my poor pleasure's sake to superadd
One possible finger's pressure to the weight
That turns, and grinds as in a fierce machine
This hapless kind, these pariahs of the sex —

Spirit  Well; people talk — their sentimentality.
Meantime, as by some sad fatality
Mortality is still mortality;
Nor has corruption, spite of facility,
And doctrines of perfectibility
Yet put on incorruptibility,
As women are and the world goes
They're not so badly off — who knows?
They die, as we do in the end;
They marry; or they — *superintend*:
Or Sidney Herberts sometimes rise,
And send them out to colonize.

126

*Dips.* Or could I think that it had been for nought
That from my boyhood until now, in spite
Of most misguiding theories, at the moment
Somewhat has ever stepped in to arrest
My ingress at the fatal-closing door,
That many and many a time my foolish foot
O'ertreading the dim sill, spite of itself
And spite of me, instinctively fell back.

*Spirit* Like Balaam's ass, in spite of thwacking,
Against the wall his master backing,
Because of something hazy stalking
Just in the way they should be walking —
Soon after too, he took to talking!

*Dips.* Backed, and refused my bidding — Could I think,
In spite of carnal understanding's sneers,
All this fortuitous only — all a chance?

*Spirit* Ah, just what I was going to say;
An Angel met you in the way!
Cry mercy of his heavenly highness —
I took him for that cunning shyness.

*Dips.* Shyness. Tis but another word for shame;
And that for Sacred Instinct. Off ill thoughts!
Tis holy ground your foot has stepped upon.

*Spirit* Ho, Virtue quotha! trust who knows;
There's not a girl that by us goes
But mightn't have you if she chose:
No doubt but you would give her trouble;
But then you'd pay her for it double.
By Jove — if I were but a lass,
I'd soon see what I'd bring to pass.

*Dips.* O welcome then, the sweet domestic bonds,
The matrimonial sanctities; the hopes
And cares of wedded life; parental thoughts,
The prattle of young children, the good word
Of fellow men, the sanction of the law,
And permanence and habit, that transmute

127

Grossness itself to crystal. O, why, why,
Why ever let this speculating brain
Rest upon other objects than on this?

Spirit      Well, well — if you must stick perforce
            Unto the ancient holy course,
            And map your life out on the plan
            Of the connubial puritan,
            For God's sake carry out your creed,
            Go home and marry — and be d – – – – d.
            I'll help you.

Dips.                    You!

Spirit                        O never scout me;
            I know you'll ne'er propose without me.

Dips.  I have talked o'ermuch. The Spirit passes from me.
       O folly, folly, what have I done? Ah me!

Spirit      You'd like another turn, I see.
            Yes, yes, a little quiet turn.
            By all means let us live and learn.
            Here's many a lady still waylaying,
            And sundry gentlemen purveying.
            And if 'twere only just to see
            The room of an Italian *fille*,
            'Twere worth the trouble and the money.
            You'll like to find — I found it funny —
            The chamber *où vous faites votre affaire*
            Stand nicely fitted up for prayer;
            While dim you trace along one end
            The Sacred Supper's length extend.
            The calm Madonna o'er your head
            Smiles, *col bambino*, on the bed
            Where — but your chaste ears I must spare —
            Where, as we said, *vous faites votre affaire*.
            They'll suit you, these Venetian pets!
            So natural, not the least coquettes —
            Really at times one quite forgets —

128

Well, would you like perhaps to arrive at
A pretty creature's home in private?
We can look in, just say goodnight,
And, if you like to stay, all right.
Just as you fancy — is it well?

*Dips.* O folly, folly, folly! To the Hotel!


SCENE III — THE HOTEL

*Dips.* And I half yielded — oh, unthinking I!
Oh weak, weak fool! Alas, how quietly
Out of our better into our worse selves,
Out of a true world which our reason knew
Into a false world which our fancies make
Down the swift spiral opening still the same
We slide and never notice. Oh weak fool!

*Spirit* Well, well — I may have been a little strong,
Of course, I wouldn't have you do what's wrong.
But we who've lived out in the world, you know,
Don't see these little things precisely so.
You feel yourself — to shrink and yet be fain,
And still to move and still draw back again,
Is a proceeding wholly without end.
If the plebeian street don't suit my friend,
Why he must try the drawing room, one fancies,
And he shall run to concerts and to dances!
And, with my aid, go into society.
Life little loves, 'tis true, this peevish piety;
E'en they with whom it thinks to be securest —
Your most religious, delicatest, purest —
Discern, and show as pious people can
Their feeling that you are not quite a man.
Still the thing has its place; and with sagacity,
Much might be done by one of your capacity.
A virtuous attachment formed judiciously
Would come, one sees, uncommonly propitiously:

Turn you but your affections the right way,
And what mayn't happen none of us can say;
For in despite of devils and of mothers,
Your good young men make catches, too, like others.
Oh yes; into society we go;
At worst, 'twill teach you much you ought to know.

*Dips.* To herd with people that one owns no care for;
Friend it with strangers that one sees but once;
To drain the heart with endless complaisance;
To warp the unfashioned diction on the lip,
And twist one's mouth to counterfeit; enforce
Reluctant looks to falsehood; base-alloy
The ingenuous golden frankness of the past;
To calculate and plot; be rough and smooth,
Forward and silent; deferential, cool,
Not by one's humour, which is the safe truth,
But on consideration —

*Spirit*                     That is, act
On a dispassionate judgement of the fact;
Look all your data fairly in the face,
And rule your conduct simply by the case.

*Dips.* On vile consideration. At the best,
With pallid hotbed courtesies forestall
The green and vernal spontaneity,
And waste the priceless moments of the man
In regulating manner. Whether these things
Be right, I do not know: I only know 'tis
To lose one's youth too early. Oh, not yet,
Not yet I make this sacrifice.

*Spirit*                     *Du tout!*
To give up nature's just what wouldn't do.
By all means keep your sweet ingenuous graces,
And use them at the proper times and places.
For work, for play, for business, talk, and love,
I own as wisdom truly from above
That scripture of the serpent and the dove;

130

Nor's aught so perfect for the world's affairs
As the old parable of wheat and tares;
What we all love is good touched up with evil —
Religion's self must have a spice of devil.

Dips.                                    Let it be enough
That in our needful mixture with the world,
On each new morning with the rising sun
Our rising heart, fresh from the seas of sleep,
Scarce o'er the level lifts his purer orb
Ere lost and sullied with polluting smoke —
A noonday coppery disk. Lo, scarce come forth,
Some vagrant miscreant meets, and with a look
Transmutes me his, and for a whole sick day
Lepers me.

Spirit          Why the one thing, I assure you,
From which good company can't but secure you.
About the individuals 't'an't so clear,
But who can doubt the general atmosphere?

Dips. Ay truly, who at first? But in a while —

Spirit O really, your discernment makes me smile —
Do you pretend to tell me you can see
Without one touch of melting sympathy
Those lovely, stately flowers, that fill with bloom
The brilliant seasons's gay *parterre*-like room,
Moving serene yet swiftly through the dances;
Those graceful forms and perfect countenances,
Whose every fold and line in all their dresses
Something refined and exquisite expresses?
To see them smile and hear them talk so sweetly
In me destroys all grosser thoughts completely.
I really seem without exaggeration
To experience the True Regeneration;
One's own dress too, one's manner, what one's doing
And saying, all assist to one's renewing —
I love to see in these their fitting places
The bows, and forms, and all you call grimaces.

131

I heartily could wish we'd kept some more of them,
However much they talk about the bore of them.
Fact is, your awkward parvenus are shy at it,
Afraid to look like waiters if they try at it.
'Tis sad to what democracy is leading;
Give me your Eighteenth Century for high breeding.
Though I can put up gladly with the present,
And quite can think our modern parties pleasant.
One shouldn't analyse the thing too nearly;
The main effect is admirable clearly.
Good manners, said our great aunts, next to piety;
And so, my friend, hurrah for good society.
For, mind you, if you don't do this, you still
Have got to tell me what it is you will.


## SCENE IV — IN A GONDOLA

*Per ora.* To the Grand Canal.
Afterwards e'en as fancy shall.

Afloat; we move. Delicious! ah,
What else is like the gondola?
This level floor of liquid glass
Begins beneath it swift to pass.
It goes as though it went alone
By some impulsion of its own.
How light it moves, how softly! Ah,
Were all things like the gondola!

How light it moves, how softly! Ah,
Could life, as does our gondola,
Unvexed with quarrels, aims, and cares,
And moral duties and affairs,
Unswaying, noiseless, swift, and strong,
For ever thus — thus glide along!
How light we move, how softly! Ah,
Were all things like the gondola!

With no more motion than should bear
A freshness to the languid air;
With no more effort than exprest
The need and naturalness of rest,
Which we beneath a grateful shade
Should take on peaceful pillows laid —
How light we move, how softly! Ah,
Were all things like the gondola!

In one unbroken passage borne
To closing night from opening morn,
Uplift at whiles slow eyes to mark
Some palace front, some passing bark;
Through windows catch the varying shore,
And hear the soft turns of the oar —
How light we move, how softly! Ah,
Were all things like the gondola!

So live, nor need to call to mind
Our slaving brother set behind!

*Spirit* Pooh! Nature meant him for no better
Than our most humble menial debtor;
Who thanks us for his day's employment,
As we our purse for our enjoyment.

*Dips.* To make one's fellow-man an instrument —

*Spirit* Is just the thing that makes him most content.

*Dips.* Our gaieties, our luxuries,
    Our pleasures and our glee,
Mere insolence and wantonries,
    Alas! they feel to me.

How shall I laugh and sing and dance?
    My very heart recoils,
While here to give my mirth a chance
    A hungry brother toils.

The joy that does not spring from joy
     Which I in others see,
How can I venture to employ,
     Or find it joy for me?

*Spirit*  Oh come, come, come! By Him that set us here,
     Who's to enjoy at all, pray let us hear?
     You won't; he can't! Oh, no more fuss!
     What's it to him, or he to us?

     Sing, sing away, be glad and gay,
     And don't forget that we shall pay.
     How light we move, how softly! Ah,
     Tra lal la la, the gondola!

*Dips.*  Yes, it is beautiful ever, let foolish men rail at it never.
     Yes, it is beautiful truly, my brothers, I grant it you duly.
     Wise are ye others that choose it, and happy ye all that can
          use it.
     Life it is beautiful wholly, and could we eliminate only
     This interfering, enslaving, o'ermastering demon of craving,
     This wicked tempter inside us to ruin still eager to guide us,
     Life were beatitude, action a possible pure satisfaction.*

*Spirit*     (Hexameters, by all that's odious,
          Beshod with rhyme to run melodious!)

*Dips.*  All as I go on my way I behold them consorting and
          coupling;
     Faithful, it seemeth, and fond; very fond, very possibly
          faithful;
     All as I go on my way with a pleasure sincere and
          unmingled.
     Life it is beautiful truly, my brothers, I grant it you duly;
     But for perfection attaining is one method only, abstaining;
     Let us abstain, for we should so, if only we thought that we
          could so.

* Cf. *Amours*, Canto III, Letter VIII.

134

*Spirit*     (Bravo, bravissimo ! this time though
            You rather were run short for rhyme though;
            Not that on that account your verse
            Could be much better or much worse.)

*Dips.*  O let me love my love unto myself alone,
            And know my knowledge to the world unknown;
            No witness to the vision call,
            Beholding, unbeheld of all;
            And worship thee, with thee withdrawn, apart,
            Who'er, what'er thou art,
            Within the closest veil of mine own inmost heart.

            Better it were, thou sayest, to consent,
            Feast while we may, and live ere life be spent;
            Close up clear eyes, and call the unstable sure,
            The unlovely lovely, and the filthy pure;
            In self-belyings, self-deceivings roll,
            And lose in Action, Passion, Talk, the soul.

            Nay, better far to mark off thus much air
            And call it heaven, place bliss and glory there;
            Fix perfect homes in the unsubstantial sky,
            And say, what is not, will be by-and-by;
            What here exists not, must exist elsewhere.
            But play no tricks upon thy soul, O man;
            Let fact be fact, and life the thing it can.

*Spirit*     To these remarks so sage and clerkly,
            Worthy of Malebranche or Berkeley,
            I trust it won't be deemed a sin
            If I too answer 'with a grin'.

            These juicy meats, this flashing wine,
                May be an unreal mere appearance;
            Only — for my inside, in fine,
                They have a singular coherence.

135

This lovely creature's glowing charms
   Are gross illusion, I don't doubt that;
But when I pressed her in my arms
   I somehow didn't think about that.

This world is very odd, we see;
   We do not comprehend it;
But in one fact can all agree
   God won't, and we can't mend it.

Being common sense, it can't be sin
   To take it as we find it;
The pleasure to take pleasure in;
   The pain, try not to mind it.

*Dips.* Where are the great, whom thou would'st wish to praise
         thee?
      Where are the pure, whom thou would'st choose to love
         thee?
      Where are the brave, to stand supreme above thee,
      Whose high commands would rouse, whose chiding raise
         thee?
      Seek, seeker, in thyself; submit to find
      In the stone, bread; and life in the blank mind.

         (Written in London, standing in the Park,
         An evening in July, just before dark.)

*Spirit* As I sat at the café, I said to myself,
      They may talk as they please about what they call pelf,
      They may sneer as they like about eating and drinking,
      But help it I cannot, I cannot help thinking
         How pleasant it is to have money, heigh ho!
         How pleasant it is to have money.

      I sit at my table *en grand seigneur*,
      And when I have done, throw a crust to the poor;
      Not only the pleasure, one's self, of good living,

136

But also the pleasure of now and then giving
   So pleasant it is to have money, heigh ho!
   So pleasant it is to have money.

It was but last winter I came up to Town,
But already I'm getting a little renown;
I make new acquaintance where'er I appear;
I am not too shy, and have nothing to fear.
   So pleasant it is to have money, heigh ho!
   So pleasant it is to have money.

I drive through the streets, and I care not a d – mn;
The people they stare, and they ask who I am;
And if I should chance to run over a cad,
I can pay for the damage if ever so bad.
   So pleasant it is to have money, heigh ho!
   So pleasant it is to have money.

We stroll over to our box and look down on the pit,
And if it weren't low should be tempted to spit;
We loll and we talk until people look up,
And when it's half over we go out and sup.
   So pleasant it is to have money, heigh ho!
   So pleasant it is to have money.

The best of the tables, and best of the fare –
And as for the others, the devil may care;
It isn't our fault if they dare not afford
To sup like a prince and be drunk as a lord.
   So pleasant it is to have money, heigh ho!
   So pleasant it is to have money.

We sit at our tables and tipple champagne;
Ere one bottle goes, comes another again;
The waiters they skip and they scuttle about,
And the landlord attends us so civilly out.
   So pleasant it is to have money, heigh ho!
   So pleasant it is to have money.

It was but last winter I came up to town,
But already I'm getting a little renown;
I get to good houses without much ado,
Am beginning to see the nobility too.
   So pleasant it is to have money, heigh ho!
   So pleasant it is to have money.

O dear! what a pity they ever should lose it!
For they are the gentry that know how to use it;
So grand and so graceful, such manners, such dinners,
But yet, after all, it is we are the winners.
   So pleasant it is to have money, heigh ho!
   So pleasant it is to have money.

Thus I sat at my table *en grand seigneur*,
And when I had done threw a crust to the poor;
Not only the pleasure, one's self, of good eating,
But also the pleasure of now and then treating.
   So pleasant it is to have money, heigh ho!
   So pleasant it is to have money.

They may talk as they please about what they call pelf,
And how one ought never to think of one's self,
And how pleasures of thought surpass eating and
      drinking —
My pleasure of thought is the pleasure of thinking
   How pleasant it is to have money, heigh ho!
   How pleasant it is to have money.

(Written in Venice, but for all parts true,
'Twas not a crust I gave him, but a sous.)

A gondola here, and a gondola there,
'Tis the pleasantest fashion of taking the air.
To right and to left; stop, turn, and go yonder,
And let us repeat, o'er the tide as we wander,
   How pleasant it is to have money, heigh ho!
   How pleasant it is to have money.

Come, leave your Gothic, worn-out story,
San Giorgio and the Redemptore;
I from no building, gay or solemn,
Can spare the shapely Grecian column.
'Tis not, these centuries four, for nought
Our European world of thought
Hath made familiar to its home
The classic mind of Greece and Rome;
In all new work that would look forth
To more than antiquarian worth,
Palladio's pediments and bases,
Or something such, will find their places:
Maturer optics don't delight
In childish dim religious light,
In evanescent vague effects
That shirk, not face, one's intellects;
They love not fancies fast betrayed,
And artful tricks of light and shade,
But pure form nakedly displayed,
And all things absolutely made.
The Doge's palace though, from hence,
In spite of Ruskin's d – – – d pretence,
The tide now level with the quay,
Is certainly a thing to see.
We'll turn to the Rialto soon;
One's told to see it by the moon.

A gondola here, and a gondola there,
'Tis the pleasantest fashion of taking the air.
To right and to left; stop, turn, and go yonder,
And let us repeat, o'er the tide as we wander,
    How pleasant it is to have money, heigh ho!
    How pleasant it is to have money.

*Dips.*    How light we go, how soft we skim,
And all in moonlight seem to swim!
The south sides rises o'er our bark,
A wall impenetrably dark;

139

The north the while profusely bright.
The water — is it shade or light?
Say, gentle moon, which conquers now
The flood, those massy hulls, or thou?
How light we go, how softly! Ah,
Were life but as the gondola!
How light we go, how soft we skim,
And all in moonlight seem to swim!
In moonlight is it now, — or shade?
In planes of sure division made,
By angles sharp of palace walls
The clear light and the shadow falls;
O sight of glory, sight of wonder!
Seen. a pictorial portent, under,
O great Rialto, the vast round
Of thy thrice-solid arch profound!
How light we go, how softly! Ah,
Life should be as the gondola!

How light we go, how softly —

*Spirit*                                        Nay;
'Fore heaven, enough of that to-day
I'm deadly weary of your tune,
And half-*ennuyé* with the moon;
The shadows lie, the glories fall,
And are but moonshine after all.
It goes against my conscience really
To let myself feel so ideally.
Make me repose no power of man shall
In things so deucèd unsubstantial.
Come, for the Piazzetta steer;
'Tis nine o'clock or very near.
These airy blisses, skiey joys
Of vague romantic girls and boys,
Which melt the heart and the brain soften,
When not affected, as too often
They are, remind me, I protest,

140

Of nothing better at the best
Than Timon's feast to his ancient lovers,
Warm water under silver covers;
'Lap, dogs!' I think I hear him say;
And lap who will, so I'm away.

*Dips.*    How light we go, how soft we skim,
And all in open moonlight swim!
Bright clouds against, reclined I mark
The white dome now projected dark,
And, by o'er-brilliant lamps displayed,
The Doge's columns and arcade;
Over still waters mildly come
The distant laughter and the hum.
How light we go, how softly! Ah,
Life should be as the gondola!

*Spirit*    The Devil! we've had enough of you,
Quote us a little Wordsworth, do!
Those lines that are so just, they say:
'A something far more deeply' eh?
'Interfused' — what is it they tell us?
Which and the sunset are bedfellows.

*Dips.*    How light we go, how soft we skim,
And all in open moonlight swim!
Ah, gondolier, slow, slow, more slow!
We go; but wherefore thus should go?
Ah, let not muscle all too strong
Beguile, betray thee to our wrong!
On to the landing, onward. Nay,
Sweet dream, a little longer stay!
On to the landing; here. And, ah,
Life is not as the gondola!

*Spirit*    *Tre ore.* So. The Parthenone,
Is it, you haunt for your *limone*?
Let me induce you to join me
In *gramolata persici.*

*Spirit*    What now? the Lido shall it be?
            That none may say we didn't see
            The ground which Byron used to ride on,
            And do I don't know what beside on.
            Ho, barca! here! and this light gale
            Will let us run it with a sail.

*Dips.*     I dreamt a dream; till morning light
            A bell rang in my head all night,
            Tinkling and tinkling first, and then
            Tolling; and tinkling; tolling again.
            So brisk and gay, and then so slow!
            O joy, and terror! mirth, and woe!
            Ting, ting, there is no God; ting, ting, —
            Dong, there is no God; dong,
            There is no God; dong, dong!

            Ting, ting, there is no God; ting, ting;
            Come dance and play, and merrily sing —
            Ting, ting a ding; ting a ding!
            O pretty girl who trippest along,
            Come to my bed — it isn't wrong.
            Uncork the bottle, sing the song!
            Ting, ting a ding: dong, dong.
            Wine has dregs; the song an end;
             A silly girl is a poor friend
            And age and weakness who shall mend?
            Dong, there is no God; Dong!

            Ting, ting a ding! Come dance and sing!
            Staid Englishmen, who toil and slave
            From your first breeching to your grave,
            And seldom spend and always save,
            And do your duty all your life
            By your young family and wife;
            Come, be't not said you ne'er had known
            What earth can furnish you alone.

The Italian, Frenchman, German even,
Have given up all thoughts of heaven;
And you still linger — oh, you fool!—
Because of what you learnt at school.
You should have gone at least to college,
And got a little ampler knowledge.
Ah well, and yet — dong, dong, dong:
Do, if you like, as now you do;
If work's a cheat, so's pleasure too;
And nothing's new and nothing's true;
Dong, there is no God; dong!

O Rosalie, my precious maid,
I think thou thinkest love is true;
And on thy fragrant bosom laid
I almost could believe it too.
O in our nook, unknown, unseen,
We'll hold our fancy like a screen,
Us and the dreadful fact between,
And it shall yet be long, aye, long,
The quiet notes of our low song
Shall keep us from that sad dong, dong.
Hark, hark, hark! O voice of fear!
It reaches us here, even here!
Dong, there is no God; dong!

Ring ding, ring ding, tara, tara,
To battle, to battle — haste, haste —
To battle, to battle — aha, aha!
On, on, to the conqueror's feast.
From east and west, and south and north,
Ye men of valour and of worth,
Ye mighty men of arms, come forth,
And work your will, for that is just;
And in your impulse put your trust,
Beneath your feet the fools are dust.
Alas, alas! O grief and wrong,
The good are weak, the wicked strong;

143

And O my God, how long, how long?
Dong, there is no God; dong!

Ring, ting; to bow before the strong,
There is a rapture too in this;
Speak, outraged maiden, in thy wrong
Did terror bring no secret bliss?
Were boys' shy lips worth half a song
Compared to the hot soldier's kiss?
Work for thy master, work, thou slave
He is not merciful, but brave.
Be't joy to serve, who free and proud
Scorns thee and all the ignoble crowd;
Take that, 'tis all thou art allowed,
Except the snaky hope that they
May some time serve, who rule to-day,
When, by hell-demons, shan't they pay?
O wickedness, O shame and grief,
And heavy load, and no relief!
O God, O God! and which is worst,
To be the curser or the curst,
The victim or the murderer? Dong
Dong, there is no God; dong!

Ring ding, ring ding, tara, tara,
Away, and hush that preaching — fagh!
Ye vulgar dreamers about peace,
Who offer noblest hearts, to heal
The tenderest hurts honour can feel,
Paid magistrates and the Police!
O piddling merchant justice, go,
Exacter rules than yours we know;
Resentment's rule, and that high law
Of whoso best the sword can draw.
Ah well, and yet — dong, dong, dong.
Go on, my friends, as now you do;
Lawyers are villains, soldiers too;
And nothing's new and nothing's true.
Dong, there is no God; dong!

144

O Rosalie, my lovely maid,
I think thou thinkest love is true;
And on thy faithful bosom laid
I almost could believe it too.
The villainies, the wrongs, the alarms
Forget we in each other's arms.
No justice here, no God above;
But where we are, is there not love?
What? what? thou also go'st? For how
Should dead truth live in lover's vow?
What, thou? thou also lost? Dong
Dong, there is no God: dong!

I had a dream, from eve to light
A bell went sounding all the night.
Gay mirth, black woe, thin joys, huge pain:
I tried to stop it, but in vain.
It ran right on, and never broke;
Only when day began to stream
Through the white curtains to my bed,
And like an angel at my head
Light stood and touched me — I awoke,
And looked, and said, 'It is a dream.'

*Spirit*    Ah! not so bad, You've read, I see,
Your Béranger, and thought of me.
But really you owe some apology
For harping thus upon theology.
I'm not a judge, I own; in short,
Religion may not be my forte.
The Church of England I belong to,
But think Dissenters not far wrong too;
They're vulgar dogs; but for his *creed*
I hold that no man will be d – – – d.
My Establishment I much respect,
Her ordinances don't neglect;
Attend at Church on Sunday once,
And in the Prayer-book am no dunce;

Baptise my babies; nay, my wife
Would be churched too once in her life.
She's taken, I regret to state,
Rather a Puseyite turn of late.
To set the thing quite right, I went
At Easter to the Sacrament.
'Tis proper once a year or so
To do the civil thing and show —
But come and listen in your turn
And you shall hear and mark and learn.


'There is no God,' the wicked saith,
  'And truly it's a blessing,
For what he might have done with us
  It's better only guessing.'


'There is no God,' a youngster thinks,
  'Or really, if there may be,
He surely didn't mean a man
  Always to be a baby.'


'There is no God, or if there is,'
  The tradesman thinks, ' 'twere funny
If he should take it ill in me
  To make a little money.'


'Whether there be,' the rich man says,
  'It matters very little,
For I and mine, thank somebody,
  Are not in want of victual.'


Some others, also, to themselves
  Who scarce so much as doubt it,
Think there is none, when they are well,
  And do not think about it.

But country folks who live beneath
    The shadow of the steeple;
The parson and the parson's wife,
    And mostly married people;

Youths green and happy in first love,
    So thankful for illusion;
And men caught out in what the world
    Calls guilt, in first confusion;

And almost every one when age,
    Disease, or sorrows strike him,
Inclines to think there is a God,
    Or something very like Him.

But *eccoci!* with our *barchetta*,
Here at the Sant' Elisabetta.

*Dips.*  Vineyards and maize, that's pleasant for sore eyes.

*Spirit*  And on the island's other side,
The place where Murray's faithful Guide
Informs us Byron used to ride.

*Dips.*  These trellised vines! enchanting! Sandhills, ho!
The sea, at last the sea — the real broad sea —
Beautiful! and a glorious breeze upon it.

*Spirit*  Look back; one catches at this station
Lagoon and sea in combination.

*Dips.*  On her still lake the city sits,
Where bark and boat about her flits,
Nor dreams, her soft siesta taking,
Of Adriatic billows breaking.
*I* do; and see and hear them. Come! to the sea!

*Spirit*  The wind I think is the *sirocco.*
Yonder, I take it, is Malmocco.
Thank you! it never was my passion
To skip o'er sand-hills in that fashion.

147

| | |
|---|---|
| *Dips.* | Oh, a grand surge, we'll bathe; quick, quick! undress!<br>Quick, quick! in, in!<br>We'll take the crested billows by their backs<br>And shake them. Quick! in, in!<br>And I will taste again the old joy<br>I gloried in so when a boy. |
| *Spirit* | Well; but it's not so pleasant for the feet;<br>We should have brought some towels and a sheet. |
| *Dips.* | In, in! I go. Ye great winds blow,<br>And break, thou curly waves, upon my breast. |
| *Spirit* | Hm! I'm undressing. Doubtless all is well —<br>I only wish these thistles were at hell.<br>By heaven, I'll stop before that bad yet worse is,<br>And take care of our watches — and our purses. |
| *Dips.* | Aha! come, come — great waters, roll!<br>Accept me, take me, body and soul! —<br>   Aha! |
| *Spirit* | Come, no more of that stuff,<br>I'm sure you've stayed in long enough. |
| *Dips.* | That's done me good. It grieves me though<br>I never came here long ago. |
| *Spirit* | Pleasant perhaps. However, no offence,<br>Animal spirits are not common sense.<br>You think perhaps I have outworn them —<br>Certainly I have learnt to scorn them;<br>They're good enough as an assistance,<br>But in themselves a poor existence.<br>But you — with this one bathe, no doubt,<br>Have solved all questions out and out.<br>'Tis Easter Day, and on the Lido<br>Lo, Christ the Lord is risen indeed, O |

[*Scenes VI–VIII are omitted*]

148

*Dips.*   The Law! 'twere honester, if 'twere genteel,
To say the dung-cart. What! shall I go about,
And like the walking shoeblack roam the flags
With heedful eyes, down bent, and like a glass
In a sea-captain's hand sweeping all round,
To see whose boots are dirtiest? Oh, the luck
To stoop and clean a pair!
Religion: — if indeed it be in vain
To expect to find in this more modern time
That which the old world styled, in old-world phrase,
Walking with God. It seems His newer will
We should not think of Him at all, but trudge it,
And of the world He has assigned us make
What best we can.
                           Then love: I scarce can think
That these be-maddening discords of the mind
To pure melodious sequence could be changed,
And all the vext conundrums of our life
Prove to all time bucolically solved
By a new Adam and a second Eve
Set in a garden which no serpent seeks.
And yet I hold heart can beat true to heart:
And to hew down the tree which bears this fruit,
To do a thing which cuts me off from hope,
To falsify the movement of love's mind,
To seat some alien trifler on the throne
A queen may come to claim — that were ill done.
What! to the close hand of the clutching Jew
Hand up that rich reversion! and for what?
This would be hard, did I indeed believe
'Twould ever fall. But love, the large repose
Restorative, not to mere outside needs
Skin-deep, but throughly to the total man,
Exists, I will believe, but so, so rare,
So doubtful, so exceptional, hard to guess;
When guessed, so often counterfeit; in brief,

A thing not possibly to be conceived
An item in the reckonings of the wise.
Action, that staggers me. For I had hoped,
'Midst weakness, indolence, frivolity,
Irresolution, still had hoped: and this
Seems sacrificing hope. Better to wait:
The wise men wait; it is the foolish haste,
And ere the scenes are in their slides would play
And while the instruments are tuning, dance.
 I see Napoleon on the heights, intent
To arrest that one brief unit of loose time
Which hands high Victory's thread; his Marshals fret,
His soldiers clamour low: the very guns
Seem going off of themselves; the cannon strain
Like hell-dogs in the leash. But he, he waits;
And lesser chances and inferior hopes
Meantime go pouring past. Men gnash their teeth;
The very faithful have begun to doubt;
But they molest not the calm eye that seeks
'Midst all this huddling silver little worth
The one thin piece that comes, pure gold. He waits,
O me, when the great deed e'en now has broke
Like a man's hand the horizon's level line,
So soon to fill the zenith with rich clouds;
Oh, in this narrow interspace, this moment,
This list and selvage of a glorious time,
To despair of the great and sell to the mean!
O thou of little faith, what hast thou done?
Yet if the occasion coming should find *us*
Undexterous, incapable? In light things
Prove thou the arms thou long'st to glorify,
Nor fear to work up from the lowest ranks
Whence come great Nature's captains. And high deeds
Haunt not the fringy edges of the fight,
But the pell-mell of men. Oh, what and if
E'en now by lingering here I let them slip,
Like an unpractised spyer through a glass,
Still pointing to the blank, too high! And yet,

In dead details to smother vital ends
Which should give life to them; in the deft trick
Of prentice-handling to forget great art,
To base mechanical adroitness yield
The Inspiration and the Hope, a slave!
Oh, and to blast that Innocence which, though
Here it may seem a dull unopening bud,
May yet bloom freely in celestial clime!
Were it not better done, then, to keep off
And see, not share, the strife; stand out the waltz
Which fools whirl dizzy in? Is it possible?
Contamination taints the idler first.
And without base compliance, e'en that same
Which buys bold hearts free course, Earth lends not
        these
Their pent and miserable standing-room.
Life loves no lookers-on at his great game,
And with boy's malice still delights to turn
The tide of sport upon the sitters-by,
And set observers scampering with their notes.
Oh, it is great to do and know not what,
Nor let it e'er be known. The dashing stream
Stays not to pick his steps among the rocks,
Or let his water-breaks be chronicled.
And though the hunter looks before he leap,
'Tis instinct rather than a shaped-out thought
That lifts him his bold way. Then, instinct, hail,
And farewell hesitation! If I stay,
I am not innocent; nor if I go —
E'en should I fall — beyond redemption lost.

Ah, if I had a course like a full stream,
If life were as the field of chase! No, no;
The age of instinct has, it seems, gone by,
And will not be forced back. And to live now
I must sluice out myself into canals,
And lose all force in ducts. The modern Hotspur
Shrills not his trumpet of 'To Horse, ToHorse!'

151

But consults columns in a railway guide;
A demigod of figures; an Achilles
Of computation;
A verier Mercury, express come down
To *do* the world with swift arithmetic.
Well, one could bear with that; were the end ours,
One's choice and the correlative of the soul,
To drudge were then sweet service. But indeed
The earth moves slowly, if it move at all,
And by the general, not the single force.
At the [huge] members of the vast machine,
In all those crowded rooms of industry,
No individual soul has loftier leave
Than fiddling with a piston or a valve.
Well, one could bear that also: one could drudge
And do one's petty part, and be content
In base manipulation, solaced still
By thinking of the leagued fraternity,
And of co-operation, and the effect
Of the great engine. If indeed it work,
And is not a mere treadmill! Which it may be;
Who can confirm it is not? We ask Action,
And dream of arms and conflict; and string up
All self-devotion's muscles; and are set
To fold up papers. To what end? We know not.
Other folks do so; it is always done;
And it perhaps is right. And we are paid for it.
For nothing else we can be. He that eats
Must serve; and serve as other servants do:
And don the lacquey's livery of the house.
Oh, could I shoot my thought up to the sky,
A column of pure shape, for all to observe!
But I must slave, a meagre coral-worm,
To build beneath the tide with excrement
What one day will be island, or be reef,
And will feed men, or wreck them. Well, well,
    well.
Adieu, ye twisted thinkings. I submit.

Action is what one must get, it is clear,
And one could dream it better than one finds,
In its kind personal, in its motive not;
Not selfish as it now is, nor as now
Maiming the individual. If we had that,
It would cure all indeed. Oh, how would then
These pitiful rebellions of the flesh,
These caterwaulings of the effeminate heart,
These hurts of self-imagined dignity,
Pass like the seaweed from about the bows
Of a great vessel speeding straight to sea!
Yes, if we could have that; but I suppose
We shall not have it, and therefore I submit.

*Spirit*                   Submit, submit!
(*from within*)        'Tis common sense, and human wit
                              Can claim no higher name than it.
                              Submit, submit!

                              Devotion, and ideas, and love,
                              And beauty claim their place above;
                              But saint and sage and poet's dreams
                              Divide the light in coloured streams,
                              Which this alone gives all combined,
                              The *siccum lumen* of the mind
                              Called common sense: and no high wit
                              Gives better counsel than does it.
                              Submit, submit!

                              To see things simply as they are
                              Here, at our elbows, transcends far
                              Trying to spy out at midday
                              Some 'bright particular star,' which may,
                              Or not, be visible at night,
                              But clearly is not in daylight;
                              No inspiration vague outweighs
                              The plain good common sense that says,
                              Submit, submit!

'Tis common sense, and human wit
Can ask no higher name than it.

Submit, submit!
O did you think you were alone?
That I was so unfeeling grown
As not with joy to leave behind
My ninety-nine in hope to find
(How sweet the words my sense express!)
My lost sheep in the wilderness?

[*Scene X is omitted*]

### SCENE XI

Dips.    'Tis gone, the fierce inordinate desire,
The burning thirst for Action — utterly;
Gone, like a ship that passes in the night
On the high seas; gone, yet will come again.
Gone, yet expresses something that exists.
Is it a thing ordained, then? is it a clue
For my life's conduct? is it a law for me
That opportunity shall breed distrust,
Not passing until that pass? Chance and resolve,
Like two loose comets wandering wide in space,
Crossing each other's orbits time on time,
Meet never. Void indifference and doubt
Let through the present boon, which ne'er turns back
To await the after sure-arriving wish.
How shall I then explain it to myself,
That in blank thought my purpose lives?
The uncharged cannon mocking still the spark
*When* come, which *ere* come it had loudly claimed.
Am I to let it be so still? For truly
The need exists, I know; the wish but sleeps
(Sleeps, and anon will wake and cry for food);
And to put by these unreturning gifts,
Because the feeling is not with me now

154

Which will I know be with me presently,
Seems folly more than merest babyhood's.
But must I then do violence to myself,
And push on nature, force desire (that's ill),
Because of knowledge? Which is great, but works
By rules of large exception; to tell which
Nought is less fallible than mere caprice.
To use knowledge well we must learn of ignorance:
To apply the rule forget the rule. Ah, but
I am compromised, you think. Oh, but indeed
I shan't do it more for that. No! nor refuse
To vindicate a scarce contested right
And certify vain independentness.

But what need is there? I am happy now,
I feel no lack — what cause is there for haste?
Am I not happy? is not that enough?

Spirit O yes! O yes! and thought, no doubt,
   'T had locked the very devil out.
   He, he! He! he! — and didn't know
   Through what small places we can go?
   How do, my pretty dear? What! drying
   It's pretty eyes? Has it been crying?

Dips. Depart!

Spirit O yes! you thought you had escaped, no doubt,
   This worldly fiend that follows you about,
   This compound of convention and impiety,
   This mongrel of uncleanness and propriety.
   What else were bad enough? but, let me say,
   I too have my *grandes manières* in my way;
   Could speak high sentiment as well as you,
   And out-blank-verse you without much ado;
   Have my religion also in my kind,
   For dreaming unfit, because not designed.
   What! you know not that I too can be serious,
   Can speak big words, and use the tone imperious;

Can speak, not honeyedly of love and beauty,
But sternly of a something much like duty?
Oh, do you look surprised? were never told,
Perhaps, that all that glitters is not gold?
The Devil oft the Holy Scripture uses,
But God can act the Devil when He chooses.
Farewell! But, *verbum sapienti satis* —
I do not make this revelation gratis.
Farewell; beware!

*Dips.*    Ill spirits can quote holy books, I knew;
What will they *not* say? what not dare to do?

*Spirit*    Beware, beware!

*Dips.*    What, loitering still? Still, O foul spirit, there?
Go hence, I tell thee, go! I *will* beware.

### (alone)

It must be then. I feel it in my soul;
The iron enters, sundering flesh and bone,
And sharper than the two-edged sword of God.
I come into deep waters — help, O help!
The floods run over me.

Therefore, farewell! a long and last farewell,
Ye pious sweet simplicities of life,
Good books, good friends, and holy moods, and all
That lent rough life sweet Sunday-seeming rests,
Making earth heaven-like. Welcome, wicked world,
The hardening heart, the calculating brain
Narrowing its doors to thought, the lying lips,
The calm-dissembling eyes; the greedy flesh,
The world, the Devil — welcome, welcome, welcome!

### from within

This stern Necessity of things
On every side our being rings;
Our sallying eager actions fall
Vainly against that iron wall.

156

Where once her finger points the way,
The wise think only to obey;
Take life as she has ordered it,
And come what may of it, submit,
Submit, submit!

Who take implicitly her will,
For these her vassal-chances still
Bring store of joys, successes, pleasures;
But whoso ponders, weighs, and measures,
She calls her torturers up to goad
With spur and scourges on the road;
He does at last with pain whate'er
He spurned at first. Of such, beware,
Beware, beware!

*Dips.*    O God, O God! The great floods of the fiend
Flow over me! I come into deep waters
Where no ground is!

*Spirit*                Don't be the least afraid;
There's not the slightest reason for alarm.
I only meant by a perhaps rough shake
To rouse you from a dreamy, unhealthy sleep.
Up, then — up, and be going: the large world,
The thronged life waits us.
                Come, my pretty boy,
You have been making mows to the blank sky
Quite long enough for good. We'll put you up
Into the higher form. 'Tis time you learn
The Second Reverence, for things around.
Up, then, and go amongst them; don't be timid;
Look at them quietly a bit: by-and-by
Respect will come, and healthy appetite.
So let us go.
            How now! not yet awake?
Oh, you will sleep yet, will you! Oh, you shirk,
You try and slink away! You cannot, eh?

Nay now, what folly's this? Why will you fool
        yourself?
Why will you walk about thus with your eyes shut,
Treating for facts the self-made hues that float
On tight-pressed pupils, which you know are not
        facts?
To use the undistorted light of the sun
Is not a crime; to look straight out upon
The big plain things that stare one in the face
Does not contaminate; to see pollutes not
What one must feel if one won't see; what *is*,
And will be too, howe'er we blink, and must
One way or other make itself observed.
Free walking's better than being led about; and
What will the blind man do, I wonder, if
Some one should cut the string of his dog? Just
        think,
What could you do, if I should go away?
    O, you have paths of your own before you, have
        you?
What shall it take to? literature, no doubt?
Novels, reviews? or poems! if you please!
The strong fresh gale of life will feel, no doubt,
The influx of your mouthful of soft air.
Well, make the most of that small stock of
        knowledge
You've condescended to receive from me;
That's your best chance. Oh, you despise that! Oh,
Prate then of passions you have known in dreams,
Of huge experience gathered by the eye;
Be large of aspiration, pure in hope,
Sweet in fond longings, but in all things vague.
Breathe out your dreamy scepticism, relieved
By snatches of old songs. People will like that,
        doubtless.
Or will you write about philosophy?
For a waste far-off *maybe* overlooking
The fruitful *is* close by, live in metaphysic,

158

With transcendental logic fill your stomach,
Schematise joy, effigiate meat and drink;
Or, let me see, a mighty Work, a Volume,
The Complemental of the inferior Kant,
The critic of Pure Practice, based upon
The Antinomies of the Moral Sense: for, look you,
We cannot act without assuming $x$,
And at the same time $y$, its contradictory;
Ergo, to act. People will buy that, doubtless.
Or you'll perhaps teach youth (I do not question
Some downward turn you may find, some evasion
Of the broad highway's glaring white ascent),
Teach youth — in a small way; that is, always
So as to have much time left for yourself;
This you can't sacrifice, your leisure's precious.
Heartily you will not take to anything;
Will parents like that, think you? 'He writes
    poems,
He's odd opinions — hm! — and's not in
    Orders' —
For that you won't be. Well, old college fame,
The charity of some free-thinking merchant,
Or friendly intercession brings a first pupil;
And not a second. Oh, or if it should,
Whatever happen, don't I see you still,
Living no life at all? Even as now
An o'ergrown baby, sucking at the dugs
Of Instinct, dry long since. Come, come, you are
    old enough
For spoon-meat surely.
                Will you go on thus
Until death end you? if indeed it does.
For what it does, none knows. Yet as for you,
You'll hardly have the courage to die outright;
You'll somehow halve even it. Methinks I see you,
Through everlasting limbos of void time,
Twirling and twiddling ineffectively,
And indeterminately swaying for ever.

Come, come, spoon-meat at any rate.
                                    Well, well,
I will not persecute you more, my friend.
Only do think, as I observed before,
What *can* you do, if I should go away?

*Dips.*    Is the hour here, then? Is the minute come —
The irreprievable instant of stern time?
O for a few, few grains in the running glass,
Or for some power to hold them! O for a few
Of all that went so wastefully before!
It must be then, e'en now.

            *from within*
                              It must, it must.
'Tis Common Sense! and human wit
Can claim no higher name than it.
Submit, submit!

Necessity! and who shall dare
Bring to *her* feet excuse or prayer?
Beware, beware!
We must, we must.
Howe'er we turn and pause and tremble —
Howe'er we shrink, deceive, dissemble —
Whate'er our doubting, grief, disgust,
The hand is on us, and we must.
We must, we must.
'Tis Common Sense! and human wit
Can find no better name than it.
Submit, submit!

Fear not, my lamb, whate'er men say,
I am the Shepherd; and the Way.

[*Scenes XII–XIII are omitted. At the end, Dipsychus has stifled his scruples, acknowledged his Spirit as Mephistophelian, and entered into a pact with him 'To own the positive and present?'*]

'I don't very well understand what it's all about,' said my uncle. 'I won't say I didn't drop into a doze while the young man was drivelling through his later soliloquies. But there was a great deal that was unmeaning, vague, and involved; and what was most plain was least decent and least moral.'

'Dear sir,' said I, 'says the proverb — "Needs must when the devil drives"; and if the devil is to speak —'

'Well,' said my uncle, 'why should he? Nobody asked him. Not that he didn't say much which, if only it hadn't been for the way he said it, and that it was he who said it, would have been sensible enough.'

'But, sir,' said I, 'perhaps he wasn't a devil after all. That's the beauty of the poem; nobody can say. You see, dear sir, the thing which it is attempted to represent is the conflict between the tender conscience and the world. Now, the over-tender conscience will, of course, exaggerate the wickedness of the world; and the Spirit in my poem may be merely the hypothesis or subjective imagination, formed —'

'Oh, for goodness' sake, my dear boy,' interrupted my uncle, 'don't go into the theory of it. If you're wrong in it, it makes bad worse; if you're right, you may be a critic, but you can't be a poet. And then you know very well I don't understand all those new words. But as for that, I quite agree that consciences are often much too tender in your generation — schoolboys' consciences, too! As my old friend the Canon says of the Westminster students, "They're all so pious." It's all Arnold's doing; he spoilt the public schools.'

'My dear uncle,' said I, 'how can so venerable a sexagenarian utter so juvenile a paradox? How often have I not heard you lament the idleness and listlessness, the boorishness and vulgar tyranny, the brutish manners alike, and minds —'

'Ah!' said my uncle, 'I may have fallen in occasionally with the talk of the day; but at seventy one begins to see clearer into the bottom of one's mind. In middle life one says so many things in the way of business. Not that I mean to say that the old schools were perfect, any more than we old boys that were there. But whatever else they were or did, they certainly were in harmony with the world, and they certainly did not disqualify the country's youth for after-life and the country's service.'

'But, my dear sir, this bringing the schools of the country into harmony with public opinion is exactly —'

'Don't interrupt me with public opinion, my dear nephew; you'll quote me a leading article next. "Young men must be young men," as the worthy head of your college said to me touching a case of rustication. "My dear sir," answered I, "I only wish to heaven they would be; but as for my own nephews, they seem to me a sort of hobbadi-hoy cherub, too big to be innocent, and too simple for anything else. They're full of the notion of the world being so wicked, and of their taking a higher line, as they call it. I only fear they'll never take any at all." What is the true purpose of education? Simply to make plain to the young understanding the laws of the life they will have to enter. For example — that lying won't do, thieving still less; that idleness will get punished; that if they are cowards, the whole world will be against them; that if they will have their own way, they must fight for it. Etc. etc. As for the conscience, mamma, I take it — such as mammas are now-a-days, at any rate — has probably set that a-going fast enough already. What a blessing to see her good little child come back a brave young devil-may-care!'

'Exactly, my dear sir. As if at twelve or fourteen a roundabout boy, with his three meals a day inside him, is likely to be over-troubled with scruples.'

'Put him through a course of confirmation and sacraments, backed up with sermons and private admonitions, and what is much the same as auricular confession, and really, my dear nephew, I can't answer for it but he mayn't turn out as great a goose as you. — pardon me — *were* about the age of eighteen or nineteen.'

'But to have passed *through* that, my dear sir! surely that can be no harm.'

'I don't know. Your constitutions don't seem to recover it, quite. We did without these foolish measles well enough in my time.'

'Westminster had its Cowper, my dear sir; other schools theirs also, mute and inglorious, but surely not few.'

'Ah, ah! the beginning of troubles —'

'You see, my dear sir, you must not refer it to Arnold, at all at all. Anything that Arnold did in this direction —'

'Why, my dear boy, how often have I not heard from you, how he used to attack offences, not as offences — the right view — against discipline, but as sin, heinous guilt, I don't know what beside! Why didn't he flog them and hold his tongue? Flog them he did, but why preach?'

'If he did err in this way, sir, which I hardly think, I ascribe it to the spirit of the time. The real cause of the evil you complain of, which to a certain extent I admit, was, I take it, the religious movement of the last century, beginning with Wesleyanism, and culminating at last in Puseyism. This over-excitation of the religious sense, resulting in this irrational, almost animal irritability of conscience, was, in many ways, as foreign to Arnold as it is proper to —'

'Well, well, my dear nephew, if you like to make a theory of it, pray write it out for yourself nicely in full; but your poor old uncle does not like theories, and is moreover sadly sleepy.'

'Good night, dear uncle, good night. Only let me say you six more verses.'

*Written almost entirely 1850–1*

# Index of First Lines